Diary of an Anaesthesiologist

Soma Kaushik

First Published in June 2021

ISBN: 978-93-5427-647-7

BLUEROSE PUBLISHERS

www.bluerosepublishers.com

info@bluerosepublishers.com

+91 8882 898 898

Cover Design:

Riya

Typographic Design:

Namrata Saini

Distributed by: BlueRose, Amazon, Flipkart, Shopclues

A Brief Foreword

I wanted to be a physician but God had willed otherwise and I instead became an anesthesiologist, a person without whom no surgery can be performed. A person who has the life of a patient in his / her hands, yet who receives very little recognition for the care given and skills employed in the most taxing and exacting surgical conditions. Many of today's medical feats such as heart, kidney or liver transplantation could not have been possible without the total dedication, skill and knowledge of the present day anesthesiologist / anesthesiologist, but can anyone recall having heard of the anesthesiologists who were involved in these ground breaking procedures? An anesthesiologist can be compared to the musicians without whom no song can be performed, yet the limelight is forever focused on the singer alone.

Every patient needing surgery requires to be anesthetized. It should be appreciated that the life of any patient hangs in balance in the hands of the person who administers anesthesia. Anesthesiologists, as we specialists are now known, are solely responsible for the successful completion of any surgical procedure from any surgical specialty, whether minor or major. The surgeons concentrate on the physical aspects of the operation, whereas we hold the physiology of the patient in our hands during the operation – the workload of an anesthesiologist is many folds more than that of a surgical specialist, not only across specialties, but right from the preoperative period (before operation) till after surgery. Once anesthesia is started all vital functions have to be continuously monitored and maintained within normal range, and after surgery the patient is brought back to consciousness. Post operatively also, the patient's care is also a continuous challenge for the anesthesiologist, who needs to supervise recovery in the ward and/or in the intensive care units.

The working hours are long, the pressure of work is far greater than that of any other medical branch, and the stress of achieving quality in each and every patient is a great a challenge - a successful anesthesiologist is a picture of total dedication, without whom none of the path breaking surgeries of today would have been possible. Although the scene is mostly dominated by surgeons, the anesthesiologist is the co-professional (akin to a musician without whom no songs can be performed) – many surgeons have been awarded high civilian honours, but unfortunately, no one knows who the anesthesiologists to those surgeons have been! I remember, Dr. Harivir Singh and I were the first to have anesthetized in the first kidney transplant at PGI, Chandigarh in 1973; the news of this great achievement was published in the front page of newspapers but we never even received a mention for our contribution. No wonder this often leads to frustration and irrevocable desperation amongst this group of specialties; Anesthesiologists also deserve the very best respect and recognition by the public, patients and the medical fraternity.

Unfortunately, there is very little awareness regarding anesthesiology, even within the medical fraternity. Nearly four or five decades ago anesthesia was often administered by technicians and untrained persons. I remember that at parties people were very keen to befriend my husband who is a surgeon, but when I would tell them I was an anesthesiologist, many would ask me if I was a doctor and whether Anesthesiologists have any special training or post graduate degrees. Many used to ask me if I made patients smell chloroform, a drug which was discarded many years ago.

The present book is a biographical sketch of a hill town girl, who against her wishes, due to circumstances, had to choose a little known medical specialty, but with her hard work and perseverance became the Chairperson and head of the department of Anesthesiology and Critical Care Medicine in the lone apex tertiary care Sanjay Gandhi Post Graduate Institute of Medical Sciences, Lucknow. The book describes her early life, upbringing, training, frustrations, trials and tribulations, as well as satisfaction in achieving recognition as a professional, who, in spite of many odds, performed exceptionally well in her many roles not only as a professional person, but also as a daughter, daughter in law, mother and loving wife.

I hope that my experiences will encourage and support a young women professionals and practicing anesthesiologists as well as women in society as well as support the cause of further development of a very important and vital discipline of medicine for the betterment and wellbeing of mankind

I hope you find it interesting.

Contents

PART 1

Early Life and Education

Chapter 1

I was born in Nainital, a beautiful hill town and the summer capital of the United Province during the British Raj (later known as Uttar Pradesh, presently as Uttarankhand). The city, also known as *The Lake City*, is situated around the beautiful bean shaped Naini lake - named after the goddess Naini, the presiding deity of the town. It sits at the foothills of Himalayas, at a height of 1938 to 2615 meters above sea level and is surrounded by lush green mountains. There are many legends and myths associated with Nainital. It is believed that there were sixty lakes around this area but forty disappeared due to deforestation. The city is said to have existed even at the time of the Mahabharat, and the Bheemtal lake nearly 20 kilometers from the town is rumored to have been created by Bheem himself to quench his thirst.

In the nineteenth century the city was discovered by an Englishman named G. W. Trail, who fell in love with the beautiful surroundings instantly. Its breathtaking beauty and pleasant weather made the city a natural choice for the summer capital of The United Provinces. Many schools and colleges were opened here for European children and it has remained an educational hub till now, the schools now serving present day elites.

My father N. C. Pant was the leading advocate of this small town while my mother, known as Kuty (which I think must be the distorted form of 'cutie'), was the one who managed the household affairs. I was the youngest of three children, with one elder brother and one sister before me. My grandmother often told us that we originally belonged to

Maharashtra, from where our forefathers migrated to escape the wrath of Muslim rulers and settled in the interior hills of Kumaon at a place called Uprara. My father's great-great-grandparents then moved to Almora and settled in a large mansion called *Jeevanpur*, our ancestral home; since then people called us *Jeevanpurees*.

One of my great-great-grandfather's brothers went to Nepal and was the Rajguru (teacher) of Nepal's royal families, however all contact with his family was later lost. I remember my grandmother mentioning him as the 'father-in-law from Nepal'. My brother was able to trace back sixteen generations of our family to our ancestors Pants who were ministers in the great Maratha ruler Shivaji's ministry. During the times of Allauddin Khilji in 1300 AD, when atrocities were being committed on the Marathas, minister Jaydev Pant along with his wife and children decided to visit the most revered deity in Badrinath in the Himalayas; on his way back he met the Maharaja of Kurmanchal (now known as Kumaon), who presented him with the village of Uprara, where they finally settled. When the family started to grow, some of the members migrated to Almora and settled in Jeevanpur.

The house at Jeevanpur is a large stone structure with more than 30 rooms, and was built by my great-great-grandfather, Jeevanand Pant. The building still stands erect even after 200 years. When I was young all marriages took place here in our ancestral house, and the whole clan collected there. It was fun to be with all the cousins, and all of us enjoyed going up and down the 72 big stone steps which connected the house to the main road.

One of my grandfather's uncles, that is, my great-grandfather's brother, Taradutt, converted to Christianity. He befriended a Christian and shared meals with him, which was considered to be a terrible offence at the time. He was labeled an outcast and refused to do penance for the 'great sin of befriending a Christian'.

His granddaughter Sheila Irene Pant married Liaquat Ali Khan in 1933, who later became the Prime Minister of Pakistan after partition. Born in 1903 in Almora my father and she studied together at Lucknow University. While she obtained a master's degree in economics my father pursued law, and they were great friends. After her marriage in 1933, she was renamed Raa'na and moved to Pakistan with her husband where she initiated many reforms for women and child development and played a major role in Pakistan politics but my father lost contact with her after she moved to Karachi.

Taradutt's family members also carried the surname Pant. One of his great great-grand-daughters Rajkumari Pant was my classmate in school and her younger sister Sheela was a year junior to us. The whole family had Hindu and Christian names and my sister and I visited them often. Most of our friends found it strange when they came to know that the two of us, a Christian and a Hindu were related to each other!

Each member of our family was highly educated and qualified. Looking back now, I realize that the only professions that I would have opted for would have been medical, legal or administrative ones.

I am not sure what profession my grandfather was in. He was in some kind of a government job and died suddenly while on transfer from one place to another in the district of Garhwal. My father was only nine years old at that time. At the turn of the century my father's uncle was a medical doctor. At a time when the country was under the British rule, it was considered a great achievement to be a doctor, especially when Indians were being looked down upon and being discriminated against. Dr. Haridutt Pant, my fathers' uncle, qualified from Lahore Medical College and was an eminent and highly successful doctor. He was a physician to Indians, Britishers, as well as to the Maharajas of Daulatpur, Vijayanagaram and Balrampur. My grandmother often claimed that it was he who was able to persuade the Maharaja of Balrampur to establish a hospital at Lucknow, known as Balrampur Hospital. It is quite possible that this is true since his photograph still hangs in the foyer of Balrampur Hospital which has now grown to be a large 2000 bed hospital in the heart of Lucknow. Dr. Pant was also very much involved in education and it was through his efforts that one of his patients - Mr. Puttulal - established the Mahila College at Lucknow, an all women school. After my grandfather's sudden death, Dr. Haridutt Pant looked after my grandmother, and it was he who helped my father's eldest brother study medicine at the same college at Lahore from where he himself had graduated.

My father was the youngest amongst his four siblings. His eldest brother was a doctor, who rose to become a 'Civil Surgeon' - the highest position in a district. The second one was the Principal at the Government College and was known to be very strict yet was very well respected as an excellent administrator. He was a strict disciplinarian; his students were scared of him, including his own children and my brother who studied at the same school. My father's third brother had been trained in textile designing and dyeing from Germany and was in great demand by most of the textile companies. He was known to chuck his job at the slightest pretext and would be taken by another company at a higher salary. He had an aristocratic living and was very fond of good food. My mother always made delicious dishes for him whenever he came to stay with us. It was saddening to see that after borrowing money from my father he refused to return it and thus came to end a healthy relationship.

My father's eldest brother Dr. B.C. Pant - whom we all addressed as Babuji - become a civil surgeon which during English rule which was an achievement not many could even dream of. He was very well known and was always being invited to royal houses and residences of senior British officers. He was very popular because he was well versed in his specialty, quick at diagnosing diseases and his treatments were always successful. He was treated like a lord even by the class conscious Englishmen. Babuji was often consulted by the family members for even minor ailments. He was a very religious man, and lived a disciplined life, getting up at four in the morning to perform 'pooja' (deity worship) for one whole hour followed by a five mile walk every day; after returning, he would have a breakfast of fruits and milk. Most of our family members were in awe of him but he was very fond of me; I was fascinated with his stethoscope, and he allowed me to play with it whenever he visited us. I also liked playing with the thermometer he carried in his coat pocket (some of them I intentionally broke so that I could get their covers!), and I would pretend to give injections and vaccinations to everyone with the outer covering of his thermometer.

Being both a physician and surgeon (as was the norm in those days), he performed all kinds of surgeries including tonsillectomies and cataracts. His operating table was a huge slab of stone, which used to be cleaned by antiseptic after every use. Perhaps the table is still there at his residence at Bareilly! There was also an ultraviolet light used for sterilization and for treatments. He often prescribed very colorful mixtures which had to be individually prepared. One particular mixture was soda salycilas - used for bringing town temperatures in case of fevers and the other for treating digestive disorders. Though these looked very attractive, their smell and taste was sickening. At that time there were no patented medicines and each mixture had to be prepared individually in a pharmacy, by people called *compounders*. One of his very effective mixtures was called 'Astringent eye lotion'. It was really astringent, and consisted of a number of ingredients such as rose water, camphor, saffron, et cetera but did cure most eye ailments.

Another doctor in the family was my cousin Charu Da, who may have contributed towards my choosing the medical profession. I do not know why but Charu da always addressed me as doctor saheba (a lady doctor) even when I was a child. He had a very attractive personality. He practiced medicine at Nainital, and looked very smart while visiting his patients on horseback, wearing breaches and a solar hat, carrying a stethoscope round his neck. I also wanted to look as smart as him on becoming a doctor. He was exceptional in diagnosing diseases just by listening to patient's complaints but he was quick tempered and disliked unnecessary questions. His medicines were very effective, his knowledge perfect and perhaps this was the reason why he did not tolerate any nonsense and had a very brusque manner. Unfortunately, he passed away a few years ago in an unfortunate and bizarre accident when a car he was standing behind suddenly reversed over him. Till the very end, he remained in contact with medical literature and was well aware of the latest developments in medical specialties. His son and I are childhood friends, and as children we played together often and even studied at the same college after high school.

Charu da always encouraged me to take up medicine as a profession.

When I was ten years old my cousin Girish da (Babuji's son) graduated as a doctor and few years Prema di, his youngest sister, also qualified as a doctor from Agra. With many doctors in the family it was but natural for me to have inclination towards a medical profession.

CHAPTER 2

My mother's side of the family was also highly educated and qualified. Most of them belonged to the legal profession. My nanaji (maternal grandfather) was an eminent lawyer and practiced in the three major districts of Nainital, Almora and Garhwal (now known as Uttarakhand). He was the government council (I think it must be something like what now is known as advocate general) for these three districts and also practiced at the High Court at Allahabad. He was a great friend of Pandit Govind Ballabh Pant who gave up his practice for the sake of India's freedom struggle and later rose to become the home minister of India. The two often met and discussed things which were beyond our understanding. Unfortunately my maternal grandfather died suddenly of cerebral hemorrhage at the peak of his career. His brother Dr. Neelamber C Joshi was a renowned surgeon who was the first fellow of the royal college (FRCS, London) from our state. He had a nursing home at Rohtak Road in Delhi, which was taken over by Delhi Government and is now known as the Dr. NC Joshi Memorial Hospital. By some strange coincidence the residence where my he had lived in, now belongs to Dr. Vinay Sabbarwal another well-known surgeon of Delhi who did his post graduate training in surgery under my husband at PGI, Chandigarh in the mid-1980s.Unfortunately Dr. Joshi was murdered during the time of partition by his own colleague Dr. Qureshi who ran away to Pakistan immediately after killing him and was never traced.

Dr. Joshi's surgical skills were known far and wide and people flocked to him from all over India. My mother often talked about him, the type of major surgeries he used to perform and how he went out of his way to help poor patients - this left a lasting impression on my mind and I could think of no other profession as noble as the medical one.

From my mother's narratives, it was obvious that when she was young, all the children in the family wanted to be like Dr. Joshi. Once such incident occurred in my nanaji's large mansion at Almora which had eight servant quarters known as "outhouses" that were just outside the main residential complex. While the adults were enjoying their siesta after lunch, all the children gathered in one of the outhouses with the idea of performing surgery like their uncle Dr. Joshi - they bound the hands and feet of one 'volunteer' and planned performing an appendicectomy on him with a kitchen knife. They were just about to cut him open when one of the elders, finding the house too peaceful, decided to visit the play place and investigate. He was shocked to see the little child bound and gagged and quickly realized what was going on. Luckily, no harm had befallen the 'patient' and all the others got such a thrashing that they never ventured to perform surgery again or even think of taking up the medical profession. But for me, rather than acting as a deterrent, such stories made medicine even more interesting.

When I was studying in class eight my mother's youngest brother D C Joshi entered for his MBBS at King George Medical College at Lucknow. Since the age difference between him and me was not much, he was more like a friend than an uncle, and he regaled us with his stories of ragging in first year, legends of ghosts in the Anatomy dissection hall, of diseases and often of hilarious anecdotes other students; they were so interesting that it made me eager to be a part of them.

Not only has this, I have often felt that the constant blessings of my grandmother also had a tremendous effect on my being choice in taking up the medical profession. Every year, her time was divided in two halves of six months each which she spent with her eldest son Babuji and her youngest son i.e. my father. Our father would go to Bareilly to fetch her, and we (my elder brother, sister and I) eagerly awaited her arrival at our house as soon as the month of April started. We always fought for a place to sleep next to her in her bed at night and listen to her bed time stories and it was I who generally had this privilege as I was her favorite. She was a beautiful old lady, with sharp features, fair complexion and silky silvery hair. She often suffered from leg cramps and my brother and I took turns to massage her legs every night and put a hot water bottle for her. In return she blessed me to be a doctor, and my only regret is that she did not live to see her blessings come true.

My father, whom we called Pappa was over six feet tall, extremely handsome and most admirable. He was a well-known lawyer who later became Government counsel and handled civil, revenue and criminal cases for the government, which brought quite a large amount of remunerations. We always felt very proud of the fact that he was very well known in the region and also was an advocate and not a 'vakil' who were supposed to be much junior and were not allowed to practice at the high court. Pappa was very fond of children and got along with them well - he never stopped us from doing anything, never scolded us, and his office drawer was always full of chocolates and other goodies - children loved him dearly. His biggest fault was that he trusted people without hesitation, to an extent that people took advantage of his 'gullible' nature again and again. We were well off, but he would keep investing money in all kinds of businesses on the 'advice' of his colleagues. Once, he put a large sum of money into the management of the reputed Waldorf Astoria hotel at

Nainital and lost it all. Then he put a large sum of money for the purchase of an apple orchard but lost that as well. However, he would never let his personal life get affected by these losses, and we never knew any want. My childhood days are the sweetest and best, and forever remain engraved in my memory.

Although we lived in a nuclear family at Nainital, my parents maintained very close ties with all family members. Summer vacations were the time when a large number of uncles and cousins descended on us. Every day, for us, was like a picnic. I now realise that it must have been quite a strain on my mother and the servants, but at that time we wished the holidays to go on forever.

Although my mother was not highly educated, she possessed wide knowledge of various topics and was a voracious reader and a strict disciplinarian and hard task master; needless to say, we were all afraid of her. She hated lies; once I told her a lie and she got so upset that she threatened to cut me into pieces with a bread knife, (I can still visualize her standing in the dining room with the bread knife in her hand) and after that, all my life I could never tell lies and was and still am quick to recognize them. Everyone called her "Chachi' which is how a younger brother's wife is addressed in India, but over the years she became a universal chachi, and everyone, including us addressed her as chachi. She was extremely good at housekeeping and fastidious about cleanliness, and our house was always spic and span. She was very particular that things had to be kept at their respective places, and we were not allowed to move anything from their places – she would immediately notice even an inch of displacement, and all hell would break lose for the culprit! She was also very particular that we should finish whatever task was assigned to us, which was difficult for me as I often left them unfinished if they were not to my liking. However, she would make me complete it and insisted that if any task is given it had to be done properly no matter how much one disliked it. She was very wary of rituals, did not believe in superstitions and was totally against any kind of God men. She did not socialize much and would not allow any idle gossip, and the impact was such that all three of us never carried tales and we were hardly ever taken to any weddings or religious festivities in other houses.

It was her upbringing and discipline combined with my father's understanding and support that helped us in becoming what we wanted - my brother joined the civil services as he always wanted, much against my father's desire for him to become a doctor. My sister was keen to become a teacher at that time, when teaching was not considered a very attractive profession but again Pappa, against all his wishes, let her train as such. I feel that both my father and mother were much ahead of their times - at a time when some families did not even allow their daughters to attend schools and married girls off as soon as they attained puberty, we were always encouraged to study and to do whatever we wished to, and take up whatever profession we wanted. Most girls at that time had no choice to decide as to what they wished to do, and a girl going out and taking up a profession against the wishes of the family, in that big bad world, was not appreciated - it was a compulsion to stay home and be at the beck and call of husbands and in-laws who were considered demigods and behaved as such, and their wives had to be subservient to their wishes.

I have very happy memories of my childhood and remember fondly the fun we had during festivals. There was no distinction between festivals of other communities. My father had a large number of Muslim clients, and during Eid they would bring us a variety of sweets and other eatables. When it was Christmas my father would send gifts and large baskets called "dalies" of fruits, dry fruits and sweets to his Christian friends. Hindu festivals were celebrated with great fervor in our community. The first was Holi, when preparations started four to five days before and special sweets called "Gujias" were cooked in very large numbers. According to tradition, at that time, men folk in large numbers from the town, collected at one place and then went from house to house celebrating the festival, playing with colours, singing and dancing to their heart's content. Our house was one such place on their route and they were served served Gujias, potato vegetables, other snacks and tea. The girls and women always stayed locked up inside the house because men were quite often inebriated with "bhang"or cannabis which is very popular during the festival.

Raksha Bandhan or rakhi was another major festival. During this, sisters tie a sacred thread (called rakhi) around the wrists of their brothers symbolizing the sacred bond between a brother and sister and the brother's duty to take care of the sister. The brothers return the love and affection by showering gifts on their sister, and at Raksha Bandhan our hands were full of rakhis. I always made sure I sat with my father and anyone who came to tie rakhi on my father had to do the same for me as well. This was also the time when Hindu Brahmins were supposed to change their sacred thread or "janau" and therefore, in the morning a priest would come to perform pooja and put a new sacred thread on my father. Although one was supposed to keep wearing it all the year round, my father would take it off as soon as the priest left since like my mother, he too did not believe in such rituals.

By far, Diwali or Deepawali was our favorite festival – this is celebrated to mark to return of Lord Rama to Ayodhya after his conquest of Raavan. During Deepawali, we decorated our house with lots and lots of colored diyas and made 'Alpana' all over the house - this is an intricate art form specially made where the deities are kept in a Hindu household. The whole house was decorated with Alpana and the feet of Laxmi, the Goddess of wealth, were painted near the entrances to the house as an offering to her to shower her blessing over the family bringing wealth and happiness. My father was very large hearted, and would buy lots of crackers and fireworks during this festival for us and for our relatives and on the day of Deepawali we would collect at the large ground by the bus stop near the lake and light them all.

There were many other minor festivals meant for either girls or for married women. "Harela" was one such festival when women and children in various houses made mud statues of God Shiva, his wife Parvati and their sons Ganesh and Kartikey. These were painted and decorated after drying and then placed at the pooja place for ten days at the end of which Pooja was performed and then they were immersed in the lake. I do not know the significance of this festival but I did take pride in showing off my handmade statues to everyone who came to our house. There were some specific festivals which were meant only for girls like "Deli Pooja" when girls got money and gifts for worshiping various thresholds at the house. What the significance of this was, no one ever explained, perhaps this meant that girls would forever take care of their parental houses. For me and my sister, the best part of all the festivals was that we always got a lot of money from my father, brother, uncles and cousins.

As I mentioned before, my parents never made any distinction between my brother and my sister and myself, and in fact my sister and I were allowed more freedom than him. The only discrimination in our house between girl and boy were perhaps during the birthdays, when there would be celebration with music and dance on my brother's birthdays, but only pooja for us on ours. There was no cake cutting or games that have now been borrowed from western culture and traditional kumaoni delicacies along with tea were served to the invitees. When we grew older, this distinction too, vanished, and our school friends (girls) would come home and celebrate our birthdays.

CHAPTER 3

Formal education in those days started from class III, and before that, most of the children were taught at home by a tutor. Our tutor was called "Pandit ji" and he took more interest in teaching my brother and sister who were already at school. He was very strict and used to hit them if they did not concentrate on their studies. I wasn't particularly interested in learning from him and he also did not bother much about me, I must admit that this arrangement suited me quite well!

My formal schooling started in 1945 when I was seven years old and was admitted to class III. At that time there were neither admission tests nor interviews with parents, and a parent accompanying any child to school was unheard of. I was taken to school by a person called "Missarji", an elderly bachelor who was also science teacher at the girl's school and was well known to my father. "Missarji" could not speak even one sentence without stammering, and we all found this very amusing and often mimicked him. Our mother always scolded us for making fun of him. It was only in later life I realized that such people needed sympathy and should not be laughed at. By the time I was admitted to school my sister was already in class five. She was a beautiful and lovable child, and a favourite of most of the teachers, which gave me an added advantage. Since there were no school uniforms in our times, our mother always dressed us in best of clothes for which we were admired by our teachers and classmates alike.

Our school was situated on a hill top and was named "Garden House", perhaps because of all kinds of beautiful flowers that grew around it. There were a large number of walnut trees in the compound, and it was fun to climb them during recess and to hide and run away when the gardener came to shoo us away. Since the school was situated on a hill top, there was no question of a school bus and every day we had to walk to the school from our house. One could, however, go on horseback, but it was fun to walk with the other girls. Every morning all of us collected at a particular spot from where we were made to walk in two rows, with the youngest girls in front and the eldest behind. At every ten yards there were maids called "Daais". Our maid was called Tulsi, and although she was very loving and kind, she was also very strict and made sure that no girl walked out of line. On the way to school, some of our teachers would join us, and we would walk together on the lane meant for horses ('ghora' road); since India was under British rule at the time, we were not allowed to walk on the main road called "The Mall", and it was only after we got our independence that Indians were able to walk there.

I soon became popular with a number of teachers. Miss Patrick who taught us English was also the class teacher of class X, where she would also teach the girls first aid. She always took me to these classes as a volunteer patient where the girls would make me lie down and tie different types of bandages, feed me soups made by them through feeding cups, etc. The whole atmosphere was of a make believe hospital. Attending these first aid classes, I also became an expert in tying bandages and could easily detect mistakes of the senior girls, and they all treated me like a VIP since my comments about the diet and bandages mattered to them for securing good marks. I am sure these first aid classes also influenced my mind for taking up the medical profession.

I am really grateful to my teachers, all of whom made me what I am today. My sister and I always remembered our teachers like Miss Patrick, Mrs. Dhyan Sundari, Miss Tripathi,

Mrs. Guruani, Mrs. Rautela etc. It is amazing that even today I remember by heart some of the lessons taught by our Hindi and English teachers. They were not just good teachers but they treated us like their own children, and did not hesitate in punishing us if we were caught doing mischief! I do not have much recollection of our principal of those days except that she was called Mrs. Mahmood whose son Tapus often came to our class and was pampered by teachers and senior girls alike. I fondly remember our principal of later years, Mrs. P Manohar Lal, who was a dynamic person and much ahead of her times; she started all sorts of activities in the school like Yoga, gymnastics, basketball, cricket kathak, bharatnatyam (Indian classical dances) etc. routinely.

At school I was often chosen to participate in sports, dramatics, music, dance etc. and my first participation in drama was soon after joining class III, when I acted the role of Rohitash, son of Lord Buddha, in "Mahatma Buddha". We were taught Kathak by Shanno Maharaj who perhaps was the cousin of well-known Shambhoo Maharaj and Bharat Natyam by Bhomla ji. We even played baseball, a game not usually played in India. Mr. Manohar Lal, husband of our principal, was an orphan, who had been brought up by my maternal Grandfather, but later, the family lost contact with him. He was an excellent painter and some of his paintings were in my mother's possession for a long time. Their youngest daughter Amita was my classmate and friend, but we lost contact with each other once I joined medical college.

We were made to participate in declamations, debates, essay writing, poetry recitation and extempore debates. One very popular activity was "Antakshari", a poetry recitation contest where the opposite team members had to start a poem from the last word the previous team had said. It was a totally literary event and not related to film music as is the custom today. In class VIII some of us went to Meerut to participate in the St John Ambulance Association first aid competition where our school stood first amongst a large number of participants from all over India and five of us (all close friends) received Gold Medals and numerous gifts. I found it really exciting to participate in all school activities, and although my mother was not happy about so many of my extracurricular activities, but she never stopped me from taking part in them.

When I was ten years old, my cousin's son PK and I were chosen to garland Jawaharlal Nehru, the then prime minister of India, on his visit to Nainital. We both had lunch with him at The Grand Hotel and also traveled with Indira Gandhi in her car upto the venue in the Flats where Nehru ji delivered his speech. We were both made to sit on the dais behind him, and I was the school VIP for quite a few weeks after this event. Till today I treasure the autograph which he signed for me.

My brother and sister always excelled in their studies whereas my rank in class was generally 5th or 6th. I was always afraid and in awe of my brother who, although only five years older than me, seemed much older at the time. He was very bright and excelled in his studies especially in mathematics; after my examinations, he would always wait for me at the front door of our house to see the question papers and check my answers. By design I would lose them, especially of mathematics in which he excelled, since I very well knew that he would immediately pick up my mistakes.

In class VIII, my friends Madhu, Bimla and I started coming home by boat every evening after school, slipping away from the usual school lines that I have earlier narrated. It was only many years later when I started rowing in front of my mother that I told her how we three had learnt to do so. As a child one doesn't even think of serious accidents which can take place with such activities!! However, since I had stood first in my class and now was doing as well as my other siblings, I got away only with a scolding; it was probably the only time I have seen my mother at a loss for words.

In March 1952, in class IX, we had to decide regarding choice of subjects; since by this time, I had decided that I would become a doctor, I opted for Science which was essential for a medical career. During school holidays during the class X UP Board examinations, I was urgently summoned to school through our science teacher with a letter addressed to my father by the Principal. I was very sure that I had done nothing wrong but my father enjoyed trying to scare me by saying that I was to be punished by the Principal and did not divulge the contents of the letter. It was only after he had had his fun that Pappa revealed that there had been an accident and two of the exam going girls had broken their arms; I was required to be the exam writer for one and my friend Sushma for the other. Sumitra, my 'candidate', was in agony because of her broken arm and was not able to dictate much; however I was able to answer most of the questions myself and even our teachers also helped on a few occasions till all examination papers were over. When the results came, Sumitra passed with distinction. It, is although, a different matter that she failed thrice in her twelfth class examinations and for a long time everyone told me that it was only due to me that she had passed her tenth examination in the first attempt!

I finished school in 1953; Mrs. Manohar Lal wrote few sentences in her own handwriting, in my praise, on the usual school leaving certificate, which I still treasure. Unfortunately, the same year, my father had an accident and broke his femur in three places. There was no orthopedic surgeon in our small town, and my brother, who was only 19 at that time, was able to get a well-known surgeon from a nearby Medical College to treat my father. Unfortunately, we were fleeced by him and went through a lot of hardship and financial difficulty as my father could not attend courts and had to undergo numerous operations before he could stand on his feet once again. This made my resolve even stronger to become a doctor and be of service to humanity.

Since the Girls College at Nainital did not have any facility for teaching Science subjects to class XI and XII students, anyone girl wishing to study science had to join the boy's college. Co-education in our times was not popular and in fact was looked down upon, and girls studying with boys were considered to be too broad minded and forward. Those were the times when many families did not allow girls to even go to school, with the ultimate aim to marry them off as soon as possible. Many did not even allow girls to come out in front of boys and studying along with them could not even be dreamt of. My own classmate and friend Kaushalya was married after clearing high school at the tender age of fifteen! Fortunately for me, my parents were very different and did not have such views, and I was allowed to join the Government College for boys without any fuss.

At college, in eleventh class, there were nearly three hundred students divided into three sections. Our biology class had 97 boys and just three girls, Pushpa Awasthi, Champa Shah and I, and the three of us always stuck together. I often wonder sometimes as to where they are now; we had kept in touch for a long time but lost contact after I went to England. The three of us occupied seats in the front row of the class, and all the boys were very decent and never bothered us. There was no question of eve teasing. Perhaps this was the best point of a small town where everyone knew everyone else and most were concerned about keeping the good name of their families intact. The atmosphere was pleasant and we never felt like outsiders, and even in the Boy's college, I was the student chosen for all intercollege or university debate contests. Nand Prasad was my partner in these competitions, and we were very successful and won a large number of trophies for the college. I am given to understand that our photographs with trophies still adorn the college walls. Nand Prasad was an excellent orator and also the topper of the physics section of our class, and all our teachers thought that he would take up Engineering; to everyone's surprise, he chose to become a lawyer, making use of his oratory skills. However, the real credit of success of my debates should go to my elder sister Uma and her close friend Birjees Begum who spent many hours in the library working out the details of the topic of the debates and writing them, unlike Nand Prasad who was a gifted orator. Even later, whenever I visited Nainital, Nand Prasad and I always met and reminisced about the good old days; unfortunately, he passed away few years back.

It is true that the boys do not take kindly to girls if their performance is better than them and my first experience of this was when I topped in chemistry and biology in my class in the final exams. Our Principal Dr. Parti was also the Professor of Chemistry, and the boys complained to him regarding my marks, that the chemistry teacher had been partial to me. Dr. Parti, at their behest, personally reassessed my exam answer book, and to their surprise and horror, gave me five additional marks after which the boys could complain no more.

By the time I was in class twelve, I was determined to become a doctor, that too, a physician and all my books had MBBS, MRCP written after my name. After passing my twelfth exam I was forced to do one year of B.Sc. because I could not appear in the medical selection examinations due to my father's fracture and treatment. By this time the number of girls in my class had risen to ten, and we now had our own group and activities; by now parents were beginning to relax their holds on daughters, thinking of quality education and many of them now allowed their daughters to join co-educational colleges. Girls had started appearing for IAS exams, but entry to engineering colleges was still barred.

I do not know why, but my teachers had great faith in my capabilities. Dr. G C Upreti, our zoology teacher once asked us all as to what our aim in life was and a number of us said that we wanted to be doctors. He then told the class that only two of us - Rajendra Gangola and I- would become doctors and rest of the students would be selling peanuts. Though his prophecy regarding both of us turned out to be true, a large number of my other class fellows also took up the medical profession and veterinary sciences as well as. Many became very successful engineers, police and administrative officers. Rajan (Dr.Rajendra Gangola) is now settled in London and we always used to meet up whenever possible.

Chapter 4

I was very keen to try the qualifying test of premedical entrance after finishing the first year of B.Sc. but my father wanted me to complete the degree before appearing for the test. He blackmailed me by saying that if I did not listen to him he would allow me only one chance to appear for the premedical test for selection to medical studies, but if I was willing to wait another year then he would let me try as many times as I wished. I was adamant and willing to take the chance, and with great reluctance he let me take the test.

At that time there were only two medical colleges in our state, one at Lucknow and the other at Agra, with only 150 total seats out of which 35 were for girls from all over India. The admissions were based on written test, for which four to five thousand students appeared; the competition was tough and admissions were based on merit in the premedical test. When another medical college started at Kanpur the number of seats rose to 250 in the state – there were a small number of seats available and it was not very easy to get admission into medical colleges even if one worked very hard for it. Fortunately for me, I qualified in the first attempt in 1956 and was selected to GSVM Medical College, Kanpur, attached to Lucknow University; this was a new college and ours would be the second batch.

I was the second girl to have been selected from Nainital and from my own family, also the second from the three districts of Uttaranchal. The first was Sushila Sanwal who married a politician who later became the Chief Minister of UP - a large Sushila Tiwari hospital was built in Nainital district in her memory, which has now become a medical college. When I got selected many people tried to dissuade my parents from sending me to medical college so far away from home. The general impression was that once in medical college, girls became too independent and did not remain under the thumb of their parents. Another, very specific reason was my cousin Prema, the first woman doctor from our family, who had recently married a Muslim boy against the wishes of her family. This had been a great shock for the Hindu Brahmin community and many 'concerned' family members hinted at this kind of possibility in my case as well. However, my parents were very liberal and were more concerned about the education of their daughters than their marriage prospects and decided to send me to Kanpur. Looking back with greatest regard, I realize their farsightedness which helped me to achieve my dreams; I was happy that my mother had the satisfaction of seeing me as the head of the largest department at the well-known tertiary care Sanjay Gandhi institute of Medical Sciences, Lucknow during my career.

My brother and Mamaji (maternal uncle) accompanied me to Lucknow for admission since the college building at Kanpur was not ready and all students were being accommodated at King George's Medical College at Lucknow. After the formalities were done, I was allotted a room at the new hostel with another student - Pushpa Sharma, who was from Jammu and Kashmir. We became good friends; later in life, her son Palash Sen became a renowned Indian singer.

I had heard a lot about ragging in medical colleges, and as first year students we were all very scared of our seniors who were ready to pull our legs anytime. But as we slowly discovered, ragging was simple - we had to sing, dance, jump, cry, somersault on demand, and mostly serves as a means of getting to know our seniors better. For boys the ragging was a little more severe - some were given a red rose and asked to propose senior girls; some were taken to movies and made to sit with their backs to the screen and everyone in the theatres laughed at them. While everyone watched the movie, they could only listen to the dialogues. Some were even paraded in the main market smoking five to six cigarettes at the same time or with their jackets worn inside out. The tradition was well known in the city and most people seemed to enjoy it. Even though we were made to perform a number of silly and stupid acts, we never came to any harm. Unfortunately, over a period of time, this pleasant interaction deteriorated to such an extent of physical and mental abuse that it had to be banned by the Supreme Court of India.

All ragging stopped after two months and we were formally 'inducted' into the fold of medical students and this was marked by a tea party hosted by our immediate seniors. The senior girls looked after us well in the hostel, and even outside, taking us out on Saturday evenings - there was an unwritten code of conduct regarding payments, and by tradition the juniors were not allowed to pay for anything if any senior was with them.

For all the glamour surrounding medical studies, students were not allowed in the vicinity of a hospital or patients at that time. For the first two years, we were expected to learn about the basics of medical practice on dead bodies (cadavers). There were only two subjects that we had to study in these first two years i.e. Anatomy and Physiology. Some of our teachers were very strict and did not spare anyone if our assignments were not completed in time, and we were really scared of some of them.The biggest terror was Dr. HC Varma, our head of Anatomy department who, we felt, derived pleasure in torturing the students, specially the girls by his acrimonious comments. He had a beautiful wife and the rumour spread around to justify his dislike for girls especially those who were nice looking was that she was having an affair with some other departmental head! Thankfully, our interaction with him was limited, and we were mainly taught by demonstrators, the junior most doctors in any department.

For learning human anatomy we had to dissect human body parts in the dissection hall. This was a huge hall with large number of marble tables on which were placed cadavers in different stages of dissection. In the morning, first year students performed dissections and in the afternoon, it was the turn of second year students. All students were allotted seats at different tables and each table was shared by eight students who dissected the cadavers. In the beginning we were allowed to dissect the upper and lower limbs only, and initially, I was made to share a table with some students who were known to notorious; as soon as one of the demonstrators Dr. Pande saw this, he immediately changed my table.

My dissection partner was SBL Garg who thought that boys were superior to girls, and no one liked his attitude. I never did dissections with him instead worked with Aisha Majeed; we got on well with each other. Aisha was a very staunch Muslim girl, and during the Ramzaan, she always fasted. Before starting her fast she used to have a sumptuous meal called "sahri" in the morning that was sent by her parents who also lived in Lucknow, and I and other friends often had a share of these tasty snacks. In the evening, during "iftar" she would break her fast with almond containing dates brought from Saudi Arabia. Later, when her two brothers got married we had the experience of a typical Muslim wedding and feasting at her home.

Initially we had no clue as to how to perform dissection, and were guided by our demonstrators as well as books called dissectors that were in six parts and our constant companions till we cleared anatomy examinations. Luckily, I did not have to purchase the dissectors since I received them from my mamaji free of cost. Every fortnight, we had table viva in which the teachers would assess how much we had learnt and how clean our dissection was, and it was only at this time that we pretended to be doing dissection with our allotted partners so that our teachers would not come to know that we were not working with them.

The second subject that we had to study in the initial two years was Physiology. This is the subject where future doctors learn of the functioning of various body systems. Our head of Physiology was Dr. UC Bhardwaj who was in total contrast to our Anatomy head; he was a likable person, a thorough gentleman and always helpful. Our practical experiments were mainly done on frogs, and we had to destroy the brains of live frogs before doing experiments on them. At that time none of us thought that we were being cruel; for us it was just a learning process, but now when I see a frog it gives me a creepy feeling!! Sometimes when the frogs were very big and slippery they jumped out of student's hands, there was great commotion and shrieks from the girls - quite often this was a deliberate act by the boys which they seemed to enjoy!!

In the first year there were no university examinations, so this was the year we all enjoyed most. Catering in the girl's hostel was excellent the mess was run by the senior girls themselves with the help of mess servants. The meals we got were sumptuous and had a choice of many dishes. The mess however was closed on Saturday evenings and we had to per force go out for dinner, which in any case we all enjoyed. Mamaji (my maternal uncle, who as I have mentioned earlier, was our age), who by now was in the fourth year of medical college, often took me out to Kwality Café or to movies and also kept a close watch on all my movements, probably at the behest of my mother. I had to inform him every time I was going out with my friends, and because of me he also became a mamaji to all my classmates. After completing his MBBS, he qualified his masters in General Surgery and then joined the Indian railway health services, later to retire as the director of railway's health services.

CHAPTER 5

In 1957, the medical college building was ready, and we moved to Kanpur. The college had been named Ganesh Shankar Vidyarthy Memorial (GSVM) Medical College in the memory of freedom fighter Ganesh Shankar Vidyarthy who was born in Kanpur and lost his life during a communal riot. It was a pleasure to sit in clean class rooms that had been recently constructed; the furniture was new and the entire building had been freshly painted few days back. There were lifts to go up and down the floors and this was a novelty for us, because such a facility was not available anywhere else. The number of students was small, and all the teachers knew us all by our first names and anyone absent was immediately noticed; none of us could afford to miss any class.

The Girl's Hostel was not fully operational, and therefore, we were accommodated in the nurse's hostel attached to Lala Lajpat Rai Hospital, where the rooms were spacious and had attached bathrooms. My immediate neighbors were senior girls Vidya and Vasantika ji, and my roommate was Indu Mathur, who belonged to Kanpur; our weekend visits to her house were a real treat because we got to eat home cooked food. After a stay of a few months at the nurse's hostel, our own hostel on the college premises opened, and we moved in there. Unfortunately, here the rooms were much smaller and had to be shared between two girls - I was allotted a room with my classmate Savita, and although initially I missed being with Indu, but over time we became fast friends and our bond has endured over than six decades since.

The hostel rooms were absolutely new and clean, and like my mother. I too had inherited her fetish for cleanliness. Fortunately, Savita was also a very neat and tidy person, and we were awarded 1st prize for the best kept room for three years running. We had a continuous water supply in clean bathrooms and uninterrupted electricity supply, but over the years, things seem to have gotten worse and now, the same hostel seem to be in a state of decay.

Pervin was another girl with whom I became good friends. She belonged to very well-known family of Lucknow and her grandfather was a renowned judge; even today Niamatullah road that was named after him exists near Aminabad. Deepali, Indu, Chaya and Chander were some other friends, but Pervin, Savita and I always moved together whether it was a movie, outing or shopping etc. and we were nicknamed 'trinity' by our colleagues.

As time went by we also started coming in contact also with the realities of life. One of our classmates was a very good singer; whenever our teachers were delayed everyone would ask him to sing, and we enjoyed his melodious songs. Unfortunately, one day he suddenly lost his eyesight and became totally blind due to retinal vein thrombosis, and could not pursue his medical studies any further. However, he was a fighter, and showed exceptional courage by studying law and becoming a renowned lawyer at Allahabad High Court.

Our Head of Anatomy was now Dr. KB Singh who was a contrast to our previous head, Dr. Verma. He was a soft spoken person, but there was something in his behavior that we could not decipher; with his blue grey eyes he looked little strange and reminded me of the priest from the novel Jamaica Inn by Daphne Du Maurier. He was always willing to help, especially girls and was even willing to clear doubts at his home. We were all very naïve, never understood his actual designs, but luckily never went to either his office or home for help. It was only a few years later his intentions became clear when the first and second year students of GSVM went on strike due to his sexual advances towards many female students and he was suspended and thrown out of college.

By 1958 we were all in third year and started classes in medicine, surgery, and other clinical subjects. Till now we had been studying what are known as non-clinical subjects which deal with body structure and functioning. Now, we came in contact with patients and felt like doctors; we all had purchased stethoscopes that adorned our necks to show everyone that we were doctors. The brands of stethoscopes that were most popular were BD and Thackray's and the ultimate was a Littman stethoscope which I purchased many years later in England. All of us felt extremely proud to be addressed as doctors, but by the end of about three months we were all beginning to suffer from all kind of diseases. One of my friend had diagnosed herself to be suffering from some kind of rare tumor, another had angina pectoris a third one had endometriosis. Students posted in surgical clinics thought they were suffering from goiters, intestinal obstructions, kidney stone or hernias. As for myself I was quite sure that I had a brain tumor because of repeated attacks of migraine. There was some sort of epidemic going on in the whole class and all of us had symptoms of some disease or other; surprisingly no student had the same disease and none of us was ever admitted to hospital for treatment. This phenomenon as my "Mamaji' told me later was called "third yearitis", when students diagnosed their own diseases based on what they were reading or coming across. Thank God none of us needed any psychiatric consultation, and by the time the third year was over we all started to be normal once again.

The whole class had been divided in four batches and we were posted either in medicine or surgery. Some of us were to attend OPDS and some had to be in the wards. Each student was allotted five patients, we had to take their history, examine them, suggest investigations and discuss them with the teachers when they came for their ward rounds, and also had to be prepared to be thrown out of the wards in case the bosses did not appreciate our efforts. We were all enamored by some of our teachers in medicine like Drs. Paul, Sikka, Jain, BL Agrawal who were excellent teachers and good human beings.

With time we became good at diagnosing diseases just based on patient histories and clinical signs. One of my aunts had had repeated abortions but no one so far had paid any attention to this. I must say I felt very proud to have diagnosed her as having Rh negative blood group and my diagnosis turned out to be correct when she was finally tested. I also diagnosed a syphilitic child and my teachers were impressed.

One class we all abhorred in our third year of college was that of our head of Pathology Prof. Tyagi. He was a very well-known pathologist but, unfortunately, was an extremely poor teacher. He used to start a topic, mix up many issues and end up somewhere totally unrelated. On top of this, he was a terror, and failed the students on the smallest pretext; as a result we were all very scared of him and dared not miss his classes. The boys in our class were intelligent but quite mischievous too, some of them would lie down on the benches and go off to sleep after attendance. Dr. Samuel and Dr. Navani were the two other teachers of Pathology whose classes we all enjoyed since they made even the most difficult topics very simple to understand whereas Dr. Tyagi made the easiest lessons difficult to comprehend. Both Navani and Samuel were young, handsome and smart and were popular amongst students especially girls.

Dr. S S Mishra our Pharmacology head was another person we all were terribly scared of. He knew each one of us by name and kept a close watch on all our activities, professional or otherwise. He was a wonderful teacher and made the subject of pharmacology very interesting, and I feel that it was the interest in pharmacology generated by him, which in later years helped me to understand the subject of Anesthesiology and the mechanism of action of drugs well. His brother Shashi Bhushan was our classmate and took part in all kinds of pranks but never conveyed anything to him including the terrible abuses hurled by students on Dr. Misra for his strictness.

Dr SK Jain, Dr. KK Sikka, Dr. Paul were our some of our great teachers in the department of Medicine. Professor BL Agrawal was our idol and we all worshiped him, not only as an extraordinary teacher but also as a person who understood the needs of his students. Dr. Paul was admired by all for his interesting lectures. He was very handsome and most of the girls admired him. When he left India and settled in USA, all of us were heartbroken and were sorry to bid him good bye.

There was one particular subject that we all had fun in - that of social and preventive medicine (SPM), and no one ever missed it. In those days this department was virtually nonexistent and all the classes were taken by persons employed in social welfare department as health officers. Generally these people were not very good teachers. Our SPM teacher was an old man and was addressed as Babuji (father) by everyone; he had no control over the class, most of the students tried to pull his legs by asking irrelevant questions. Every one derived some kind of vicarious pleasure when the teacher was unable to either answer the question or could not make his statement clear. He had two sets of glasses one for the near vision and the other for distance vision. When he wore the near vision glasses he could not see the students sitting at the far benches and when he changed the glasses for the distance he could not clearly make out the students in front and we all found this very amusing. This was the only subject where during the house tests everyone went with the textbook in hand and copied the answers!

Prof. CB Singh and Prof. SP Shrivastava, our respective principals, were also the heads of the surgery department. Dr. Singh was an excellent teacher but he hardly had time to teach because of his administrative responsibilities. On the rare occasions whenever he came to teach us he was followed by a large coterie of his juniors who were made to sit amongst us. He always made it a point to insult some with whom he was not very happy that day by asking questions which they could not answer. All the students had to compulsorily attend his operating sessions, and on the first few occasions some girls and boys would always fainted at the site of blood or large incisions. He would roar at the OT staff and ask them to throw the students out. At that time we all thought that he was the greatest surgeon of his times because he hardly took any time to complete even complex surgeries! It was later in life I realized that all the preliminaries were completed for him by his juniors before he joined them in the OT. He only had to perform the removal of a tumour, Gall Bladder or an organ, which did not take very long, but as young, gullible students we were all impressed by his swiftness! During surgery one junior faculty member had to be ready to wipe his forehead if he sweated and the other had to be ready to give him a sip of water if he so desired. The patients were ever so grateful to him (the great surgeon) for operating on them, and if they recovered it was all because of him but if they succumbed even then the relations were grateful that their patient had been operated by him, the renowned one, but unfortunately, due to God's will, did not survive !!

Professor SP Shrivastava who became Principal after Dr. CB Singh was also a very well-known surgeon and had an exceptional memory. When I met him at a conference, after almost twenty years after passing out from college he addressed me by my maiden name, which was unbelievable. Although brilliant, he was short tempered, and would never pardon the shortcomings of his juniors whom he often slapped and kicked. However, at that time, no one took any offence because he was the real 'guru' who made them proficient in surgical skills, something that is unimaginable now. Those were the days when all renowned surgeons moved around with a halo round their heads and were held in high esteem, and could literally say or do anything they wanted to.

When posted in Medicine, we had to attend medical wards and had to write the medical history, diagnosis, investigations of patients allotted to us. Like in the surgical side, these had to be discussed with the teachers during ward rounds, and we all had to be ready to be skinned by them in front of the whole batch, nurses, ward boys. It would become quite insulting at times if one did not have the correct answer. Our head of Medicine was Prof. KN Gaur who was very particular regarding English and the use of appropriate words and correct grammar. He had been trained in England, and had a number of degrees after his name and made us all carry a pocket Oxford dictionary. He always made it a point to let us know during each teaching session as to how bright he had been as a young student. In my final year exam, he got annoyed with one incorrect English word that I had uttered in my viva and he stormed off saying that "if you cannot speak correct English you do not deserve to get top marks".

CHAPTER 6

Third year was considered as the year of relaxation as there were no university examinations; as a result, most of the students took the year lightly. I stood second in my class that year and also got merit scholarship, not because I had any exceptional qualities or I was a very good student but because 70% of students had failed in one subject or other! And there were very few who had been able to pass in all subjects. It though is a different matter that all my class mates whether pass or failed were promoted to the next class when the real test of our knowledge and skill was to take place at the University second professional examination.

One of the lively features of any medical college is its annual function when various competitions in games, quizzes, dramatics etc. are held for a week to ten days; for the students this was an undeclared holiday. The most important was the variety entertainment programme in which students from different classes were chosen to participate, and since the programme was usually held in the presence of some dignitary it had to be really good. The teachers would select students for the event, and it was next to impossible for any student to refuse to participate because the chairperson was one of the heads of department who could make your stay in medical college miserable. In my first year I was chosen to give a dance performance at the annual function, and this became an annual feature till I finished college. In my forth year I was very reluctant to participate due to the approaching university examinations and accordingly informed the chairperson, who did not agree. Then, I tried all sorts of measures (including a telegram from home regarding my father's illness) but all my pleas fell on deaf ears; instead I was threatened with severe consequences including failure in the final examinations, and although unwilling, I had to participate. It is unfortunate that I consider it good fortune for me that I developed enteric fever and its relapse in my final year and was hospitalized for nearly a month, thus missing the function and its preparations.

Medical studies in our times were for full five years. All my close friends and I passed out of college with reasonably high ranks. There was no internship at that time and only 30 salaried house jobs were available on basis of merit in final exams, and the rest of the students had to either work honorary (without salary) or look for jobs elsewhere. The first 6 to 7 students always were given house job in Medicine which was the most sought after specialty at that time. Fortunately, our trinity, my two friends Savita, Pervin and I got house jobs in General Medicine, and continued together. I was posted in the unit of Prof. Gaur, who was our Head of Medicine. It was considered an honor to walk beside him, and those of us who were in his unit had our feet above the grounds. However, the biggest disadvantage of working with him was that we had to listen to him blowing his trumpet day in and day out, but the advantage of learning from his experiences, excellent training and being on a superior level than your own colleagues far outweighed this!

Girls staying alone in the hospital emergency, in the doctor's duty room, was considered unsafe therefore we all stayed in the hostel rooms even on our call days. If one of us was called to the hospital for any emergency all three of us went together – not only was it safe, we also felt that three brains were better than one, since as students, we had never come across situations where independent decisions had to be made on the spot to treat people. My friends and I were only equipped with theoretical knowledge and did not know how to tackle day today problems, especially emergency situations. No doubt our individual views sometimes did clash and create confusion, but overall, the concept worked.

Since there were no telephones, the calls were sent through a messenger, and since there was no facility for hospital transport, it often led to inordinate delay with sometimes turned out to be fatal for the patient. Unfortunately our planners have never been far sighted, and I often feel that various governments have created medical institutions not out of consideration for human welfare, but to add achievements to their own credit and to ensure return to power; this is the reason that only halfhearted facilities are thought of while planning medical colleges. This holds true even today when a large number of medical institutions are opening up, without adequate infrastructure, facilities and funds.

After spending six months in the first unit I was posted with Prof. BL. Agrawal, head of the second unit. It was a pleasure working under him, not only because he was an excellent teacher, but he also because he was very considerate towards his juniors. We were not afraid of him and could approach him anytime in case of difficulty. He would often leave his lunch box for us if we were busy in wards, and kind gestures like this are always hard to forget. Due to some reason, all investigation forms had to be signed by the head of the units, and as a result of this, all of us had to learn to put the signatures of our bosses on the investigation forms. In this regard, we had their full support because they had no time to waste in signing investigation forms due to their busy private practices.

As a part of the usual rotation, after completing one year of posting, we were posted in Pediatrics. The Head of Pediatrics at GSVM Medical College, Prof. JN Shrivastava, was a learned man who had trained in England and obtained

MRCP in the subject. He was an excellent teacher and painstakingly explained many procedures to us. The other faculty members, Dr. Mathur and Dr. Shrivastava were in total contrast to each other - Dr. Mathur was tall and handsome, Dr. Shrivastava was short and dark; every day both of them sat in the busy OPD seeing children. Whereas Dr. Mathur always took a long time in examining his patients and the other took just a few minutes to come to the correct diagnosis. Dr. Mathur was also an excellent singer and after the ward rounds often regaled us with melodious songs. As a result, all three of us wanted to pursue further studies in either pediatrics or medicine, but circumstances prevented me from doing so; Savita and Pervin, however, were fortunate enough to pursue their chosen careers but and I was forced to take up anesthesiology. Pervin retired as the Head of Pediatrics from the prestigious JLN Medical Institute, Aligarh and Savita from Balrampur Hospital at Lucknow, and we still remain in touch with each other.

Family photo, with father and mother (both sitting), elder brother Satish (standing), elder sister Uma (sitting on father's lap) and myself (sitting on mother's lap)

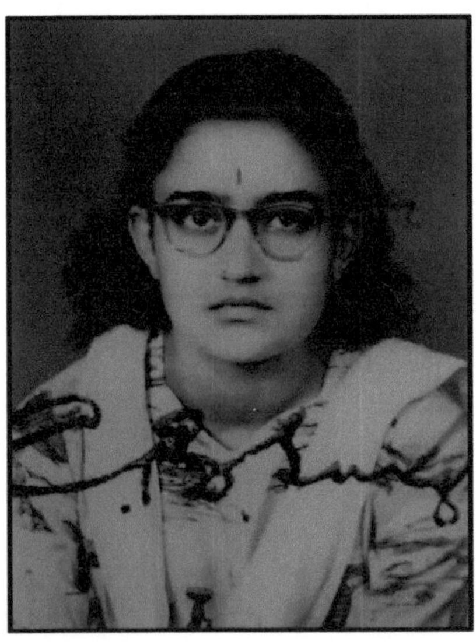

Photograph of the author during college

After marriage, with elder brother (extreme left), self, husband and elder sister (extreme right)

With husband (Satyendra) at Nainital

Ireland, with Amit (son) and Satyendra

Celebrating 25th Anniversary

DR. B. L. AGARWAL
M.D., M.R.C.P.

.M. MEDICAL COLLEGE
KANPUR

PHONE: 26137

TESTIMONIAL

It gives me great pleasure to write in support of Dr. (Mrs.) S. Kaushik whom I had known both as a student and house physician. She passed M.B.,B.S. in April 1961 from G.S.V.M. Medical College, Kanpur (Lucknow University) and secured very good marks.

As a student I found her a very keen and active person with wide interests. After graduation she worked as house physician in the Department of Medicine from June 1961 to January 1962. During this period, we were impressed by her hard work, earnestness and initiative in diagnosis and treatment of patients under her care.

I can unhesitatingly recommend this young lady doctor who in addition to her capacity to work sincerely bears a very charming and likeable personality to any post to which she may apply.

BLAgarwal

24.11.1962.

PROFESSOR OF CLINICAL MEDICINE.

Testimonial from Prof. BL Agarwal

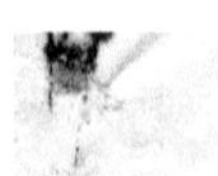

DONCASTER ROYAL INFIRMARY

TELEPHONE 2286

DEPARTMENT OF ANAESTHETICS

HBY/LFB

1st June, 1967

TO WHOM IT MAY CONCERN

Dr. S. Kaushik acted as Registrar in Anaesthetics to the Doncaster Group of Hospitals for eight months during the period from September 1966 until May 1967.

In that time Dr. Kaushik demonstrated in an impressive manner her mastery of all the Anaesthetic Techniques associated with the surgical work in a very busy general hospital comprising all the usual specialities with the exception of Cardiac, Pulmonary and Neurosurgical work. She has a pleasant manner, a likeable personality and is essentially co-operative in her attitude to Medical and Nursing colleagues.

During her stay in Doncaster she showed her capabilities by undertaking the independent anaesthetic care of large major surgical lists with equanimity, and her work was always well appreciated by even the most exacting surgeon.

In addition to the routine work of "cold" surgery, she did her fair share of emergency and accident work, and this was always performed in an exemplary manner. Throughout her work her patients were always her main care and everyone benefitted from her skill and patience.

It was a great disappointment to us that Dr. Kaushik had to terminate her engagement with us after such a short time in Doncster. We have in Doncaster thereby, lost the services of one, whom I can confidently recommend to any institution requiring the assistance of a very well qualified anaesthetist.

H. B. Young.

H. B. Young,
M.B., Ch.B., D.A., R.C.S.G.,
Consultant Anaesthetist

DRI/LH 5 ICM

Testimonial from Prof. Young

PART 2

Living and Training in UK

Chapter 7

In August of 1962, after a long courtship of 6 years and some resistance from family because of our totally different social backgrounds, my classmate Satyendra and I were married at Nainital. Satyendra was one of the toppers of our class with 13 awards and medals to his credit and had been nick named "Prince Charming' by all my class mates.

My husband was the youngest of five brothers and three sisters. My father in law was a rich zamindar family in UP and owned nearly three fourths of their whole town land; they also had many mango groves and guava orchards. He was also a well-known farmer who had been awarded the title of Krishi Pandit by the then President of India, Dr. Rajendra Prasad, for the highest yield of wheat and was often invited by various agriculture universities to give lectures on this achievement. He wore many hats, and was the also a town elder and city magistrate. Many years later, I made an album of his achievements, which unfortunately has been misplaced; maybe it is now with someone in our extended family. On his insistence, I also made a family tree which now has been updated by my husband nephews. The two elder brothers were involved in managing the farms, the next one was an engineer, and the fourth one, worked with customs and excise and later retired as the chief of customs services in India. Their family was very loving.

Satyendra had developed an interest in becoming a surgeon, and soon after our wedding, he left for England, which was then known as the Mecca of medical studies for further training in surgery. I joined there a few months later, and London, for few months was like an extended honeymoon; we went out to eat and to see various places of interest nearly every day. However, this could not last forever and I soon had to learn to manage home affairs.

Our abode was a one room bed sitter apartment in Acton Town which had been rented out to us by an Indian family related to one of our seniors from college, but we had to share the kitchen and bathroom with an Italian family. The underground station was only a two minutes' walk from the place and thus the apartment was very conveniently placed. Satyendra was already attending classes for his primary FRCS examinations, and since it was not possible for me to take up any job till this was over, I was left to look after the house (i.e. one single bed sitter!!). England, which till now had been a dream country for me did not remain the same once I got involved with mundane household chores. I had neither cooked nor cleaned dishes, and did not even know how to light a gas stove since my mother had never allowed her two daughters to even enter the kitchen - her sole aim had been to make sure that we had time to study well. As a result, I often landed in hilarious situations. Rice was like gruel, chapattis were like the Australian map, and vegetables generally remained uncooked. However, our Italian neighbor was a very helpful lady who often came to my rescue.

As soon as his primary was over, Satyendra, who by now had become Satti to all his English classmates, got an SHO job at Royal Infirmary at Stockport and we moved there. While he was working at Stockport, I got a job at Ashton under Lyne, in Pediatrics, with Dr. Hilson. Dr. Agrawal, who was registrar to the chief had been our Physiology demonstrator at Lucknow, and I felt very happy to join this unit. To my surprise he had changed – he had married an English girl soon after landing in UK, and then had begun to despise his own countrymen. Since I had to commute between

Ashton and Manchester (I was living at Manchester) every day, I decided to rent out a room in Ashton town, thus my husband and I had to live separately. However, as I also did not enjoy working here, I took up a locum in medicine at Nuneaton, a place that was more convenient to travel to. This was a small county hospital which was totally managed by Indian and Pakistani doctors and most of the junior doctors were foreigners. The atmosphere was very friendly. My Registrar was a Sikh gentleman whose son suffered from cerebral diplegia. It was an irony that a nice and dedicated doctor like him could do nothing for his own son!! This was in early sixties, and the concept of superspecialities had not yet come in. Branches like neurology, cardiology, and nephrology had not developed fully. I still remember one of my patients suffering from chronic renal failure whose blood pressure and blood urea was rising day by day because of which he was becoming disoriented, but we could do nothing for him because neither dialysis nor kidney transplantation was available.

I was extremely happy working in this hospital but the only problem with this assignment was that the hospital was again quite far away from my husband's place of work. Medicine and Surgery were the two most sought after specialities at that time, and indeed, the first preference for any such vacancies was for the whites of England. Thus it did not seem possible for both of us to get jobs in the same hospital. If there was a vacancy in Medicine there was nothing available in Surgery, and vice versa. Fortunately, we both got appointments in our respective specialities in Ireland after a few months and moved to Ballymoney, a small town in Northern Ireland. By this time I was already expecting my first child, therefore I did not join immediately.

Ireland is the most beautiful place that I have ever visited in my life. I have been very lucky to have visited many countries but there is hardly any place which can compare to the natural beauty of Ireland. It is a land of Blue Mountains, forests, parks, breathtaking natural beauty, lakes, moors and white Atlantic sand. Belfast was the largest city, but there were many small towns hidden away all over the green countryside. Ballymoney was not a big town, with a small and friendly population. The Route Hospital was the general hospital for the area with all facilities, and Mr. Martin, my husband's boss, was a pleasant man and it did not take us very long to settle down.

Since there was only singles accommodation available at the hospital, I had to stay outside in a rented paying guest accommodation. My landlady Mrs. Reed was an Irish housewife who was quite friendly and also provided meals to me, but I was not very keen on boiled food. She was an excellent cook and was especially good at baking, and taught me how to make cakes, scones, etc.; her whole day was spent in household work. To me it seemed that Irish families were also somewhat like Indians. Men folk were generally interested only in their jobs or being couch potatoes whereas the women had to slog all day long to keep the house going. The place where I was staying was quite far away from the Route hospital where I was booked for my delivery and since we had no transport we had to move to another place that was at a walking distance from the hospital. The new landlady Mrs. Dooey was also a very helpful Irish lady who looked after me very caringly when Amit, my elder son, was born. She not only gave me a room but also allowed the use of her sitting room, TV, etc., a gesture not often seen in a foreign land. Every night she took away Amit to her room and made me rest while she and her elderly husband took turns to feed and change the little baby. I cannot forget Mr. Martin, my husband's boss, who was also very concerned about our welfare. He sold his absolutely new Ford Anglia car to Satti at a throwaway price, and the car became an essential part of our life. We were really lucky to have come across such nice and considerate people like them. Recently, Amit visited the place of his birth, but found that Route hospital has now been pulled down and in its place a new housing complex has been built.

The only problem which I faced in Mrs. Dooey's house was that of a bathroom. At that time a large number of Irish Houses were without bathrooms and their weekly ritual of bathing took place in the kitchen where they used to fill up a big wooden tub and bathe in it. For me this was unheard of and I had to run to Satyendra's room in the hospital for my daily bath.

I had been offered a job in medicine and had to move to Omagh to join as an SHO at Tyrone County hospital. Amit was only four weeks old but since the hospital authorities did not want to wait any further, I had to start working at a time when most of the women in our country are looked after and pampered by their parents or in-laws. I had to part from my newborn son and leave him in the care of Mrs. Dooey who had very kindly agreed to do so, on nominal payment. Her daughter Genella also helped in taking care of my son, and my husband who was still working at Balleymoney could visit Amit often. Thus after arranging for the care of my son I moved to Omagh to work at the Tyrone County hospital.

Tyrone is a County; Counties are like our districts. The three important towns of Tyrone County were Omagh, Dungannon and Cookstown. It is known that the O'Neil's were the rulers of this county and the ancestral home of American president Woodrow Wilson is also here. The Sacred Heart church at Omagh is one of the most peaceful places to visit. It also has the well-known Neolithic sites like the Beaghmore stone circles near Cookstown and Ulster History Park which are worth a visit. Tyrone County hospital is the major hospital serving this area. In February 1964 I joined Tyrone County Hospital at Omagh as an SHO in Medicine. This was a small 250 bed hospital and the atmosphere was friendly, the nurses were helpful, and my chief Dr. Peter Tattersol, treated me like his own daughter. There were a few other Indian doctors - Dr. NR Kulkarni and Dr. Nandi in Surgery, and Dr. Kakkar in medicine. Dr. Pollock, too was, I think, in surgery, and Dr Cherian joined few weeks after me in Surgery and his wife in Medicine. The hospital accommodation was good and we were provided with sumptuous meals throughout. Dinner was served every day at 6 in the evening and supper around 10 at night. Supper was most delightful when we could have sandwiches, buns, scones, toasts etc. with milk, coffee, chocolate Horlicks etc. as drinks. Dr. Kulkarni was a vegetarian and because of him we were served Indian curries and Pulao once every week. On Sunday the kitchen was closed, so all the Indian doctors would get together, take over the kitchen and cook a number of Indian dishes, and in this Mrs. Cherian had a major role to play.

A few days after I joined, an English woman (I forget her name) also joined to do her internship in medicine. She was an elderly lady in her mid-fifties and had recently completed her undergraduate studies. She had grown up children and had started her undergraduate course late in life, but for me, it was a little embarrassing to teach the basics of medical management to someone who was double my age. But then, as I learned, learning is not age related and in England there is no age limit to get educated; many start going to university after settling their off spring.

My first patient at this hospital was a young boy of eleven years who had been admitted the previous night with breathlessness. I examined him and made a diagnosis of an ASD, a congenital heart disease, which, on further investigation, turned out to be correct. This made such an impression on Dr. Tattersol that he developed total faith in me. Before going to UK I had heard a number of stories about colour discrimination, but to my surprise the place was in total contrast, and I enjoyed working here. Perhaps we have more discriminatory feelings in India on the basis of class, creed and culture and tend to discriminate between a Punjabi, Bengali, Madrasi Malyali and so on, but the hospital atmosphere was very friendly. I also became very friendly with my ward nurses. Nursing in western countries is considered a very respectable and noble profession and a large number of nurses belong to high class and elite families. In contrast to Indian nurses, they have a much better knowledge of basic subjects such as Anatomy, Physiology and also are well versed in Medicine. They are dedicated, sympathetic and highly motivated in their line of work - I really do not remember any nurse getting impatient or angry with patients; sometimes, they are more knowledgeable and experienced than the new, young doctors just out of medical colleges, and I do not hesitate to admit that I did learn a number of tasks from them.

My other colleague was Dr. Kakkar who was a few years senior to me. At medical colleges, juniors are taught to show total respect to their seniors and do whatever asked. Dr. Kakkar took full advantage of this; being a bachelor, he would often go out on dates, even when he was on night emergency duty. He always requested, rather ordered me to look after the emergencies and like a fool I would work all night in his place. Dr. K. would come to the ward early next morning, go through the files, see all what had been done and then present the case to Dr. Tattersol during the rounds, as if he had been working all night himself. On one such night, when it was his call day one young Indian boy was admitted with severe status asthmaticus, a serious condition that needs constant supervision and care. Sometimes, they even need to be on assisted respiration through a ventilator. I had been at the bedside of this young boy all night, and by morning the child had fully recovered, but again, the same old story was repeated; Dr. K as usual took the lead and presented the case history to the chief. I felt very annoyed but did not say a word to the Dr. Tattersol. After all what could a junior do? But I was surprised when Dr. Tattersol called me to his office later and told me that he "was aware of everything that goes on in the ward and was planning not to give any extension to Dr. K".

I came to know later that it was the child's father Mr. Tandon who had communicated his thanks to my chief and praised my dedication. Mr. Tandon was a top local businessman of Omagh, and I became friendly to them. Every month, they would invite me to their home for a meal and his wife, Mrs. Tandon gave me many lessons in Indian cookery of which I knew very little. Thanks to her tutoring, I became a reasonably good cook.

Dr. Tattersol always addressed his patients by their first names and it made me realize that the patients were just not bed numbers; doctors had to be friendly and show utmost concern for their ailments no matter how simple the problems were. In India, we had been talking about patients by their bed numbers and sometimes the treating physicians did ridicule them. I am thankful to Dr. Tattersol as well as other colleagues for their lessons in kindness. Once a girl who tried to commit suicide was admitted to our ward, and with very active and timely efforts by the doctors and nurses she survived - it was a lesson in humanity to see how kindly she was treated by everyone. In another instance an old man tried to take his life by taking a large number of sleeping pills because of problems with his children who neither looked after him nor supported him financially. He too, was saved, but got very angry with all of us for saving him; he was later sent for psychiatric treatment and a place was arranged for him in an old Peoples home by social workers. It is a pity that in our country till today, suicide is considered illegal and little is done to help such persons.

Although at Omagh I was very happy as far as work was concerned, the home front was not satisfactory at all. Amit was getting repeated chest infections and pneumonias and it was becoming extremely difficult to manage him as well as continue in my chosen profession. Due to this I was quite miserable and often thought of giving up my job; my boss was a very pleasant man who did not want me to leave as he was happy with my work but he also understood the pain of separation from the family because of his own sufferings. Dr. Tattersol, it was quite often mentioned in the coffee room gossips, was a Jew who had been separated from his near and dear ones and imprisoned in a concentration camp from where he had escaped through an underground tunnel. He often allowed me to bring Amit and keep him in the ward nursery during the week ends but it was like encroaching upon his goodness and taking unnecessary liberties.

Fortunately, Dr. Khobragade, who was appearing for his FRCS examination and had become our friend while Satti was working with him at the Royal infirmary at Stockport, had also moved to southern Ireland as a registrar with his wife who had left their two young children back in India. In their absence she often felt lonely, and offered to look after Amit. This was a God sent opportunity for us and we immediately accepted this offer and left Amit with them at Moynaghen which was only two and half hours' drive from my place of work. We remain in their debt forever for their help in our hour of need. However, although Mrs. Khobragade looked after Amit as her own child, he was getting repeated chest problems and we had to rush to them often, creating a problem for us as it was difficult to take leave so frequently.

Given the situation on the family front, many of our friends advised me to take up anesthesiology as a specialty as there was a shortage of anesthesiologists in UK and jobs were available for asking and this was the only way, short of leaving my profession that the whole family could be together. Dr. Tattersol was very reluctant to let me go, and I was even more reluctant to join a specialty about which I had no knowledge. He insisted that he would not relieve me till I got some good doctor to work for him as my replacement, and I therefore recommended my very close friend Savita, who was still in India and planning to come to UK. Dr. Tattersol accepted her without any hesitation, and she also showed her mettle and Dr. Tattersol was extremely happy with her work. Savita later did her post-graduation in Pediatrics from London, and settled down in Lucknow after coming back to India.

CHAPTER 8

I was offered a SHO post in anesthesiology at Altnagelvin Hospital at Londonderry where my husband was already working, and joined there in August of 1964. I wrote to Prof. BL Agrawal, my Professor of Medicine at my college for a testimonial, and he sent me a very good testimonial but also sent a letter along with it discouraging me to take up the specialty by saying that "You would be wasting yourself by taking up anesthesiology". I was disheartened.

This just goes to show that even in the minds of our teachers anesthesiology had a very low priority. The progress of anesthesiology in India had been very slow and static and quite often practiced only by unqualified compounders, nurses and sometimes even by orderlies. By the time I entered medical college changes had started taking place and Anesthesiology was establishing itself as an independent specialty, but only those students who had no other option took up anesthesiology, whereas the brighter students took up either medicine or surgery. My own knowledge of anesthesiology was totally inadequate. As students we had just ten lectures in the subject in our final year of medical studies. We only attended those to make fun of the teacher who had been nicknamed "hanuman" (a legendary character from the epic "Ramayana", who was known to have moved mountains.). I do not know why he had been given this name, since he neither could move mountains nor could lift a finger at the students, and we learnt nothing regarding anesthesiology.

My very first encounter with anesthesiology had been in 1962 while doing a house job in Gynecology and Obstetrics. I was planning to go to UK and it was mandatory for registration with the British Medical Council to have an experience of working in at least two specialties out of Medicine, Surgery and Gynecology and Obstetrics. As a result, I took up a house job in the subject. One day my classmate Chaya and I were asked to perform tubal ligation in a woman who had delivered just three days back. Our own classmate Usha was asked to give anesthesia, unfortunately she was inexperienced and had no training in anesthesiology. In any case none of us had any clue of what anesthesiology meant. After struggling with the patient for a long time the patient was put to sleep using open drop ether, and we proceeded with surgery. A little while later I saw that the tube was a little blue and Usha was informed, but she told us to go ahead; soon the tubes became bluer and then black, we told her again and to our horror, realized that the patient had stopped breathing. She had no pulse or heartbeat and had had suffered a cardiac arrest. Immediately a senior anesthesiologist from the adjacent theater was called, he too was not very experienced and did not know what to do, and called another senior who came to the OT door, looked at the patient from a distance, screwed his eyes up rather whimsically, shrugged his shoulders and declared her dead in a dead pan flat voice saying "oh she is dead".

We were just helpless and could do nothing. Resuscitation methods were not known, no one had heard of closed chest massage. The whole episode was so scary that none of us wanted to be in such a specialty where there was such a small margin between life and death!! Even today I can visualize that dreadful scene and the thorough dressing down we got from our head, but this made us firmly decide never to take up anesthesiology as a profession.

Fate willed otherwise in my case, and equipped with little knowledge of the specialty I joined at the Altnagelvin Hospital at Londonderry and was provided a fully furnished accommodation of a two bed rooms flat with sitting and dining room and completely furnished kitchen within the hospital compound. Even the bed linen was provided by the hospital which was changed, washed and returned to us every week. We were also able to arrange for an Irish girl named Elizabeth to look after Amit. Life now was beginning to look brighter. My neighbors were Dr. Price and Dr. John, who were both friendly and helpful. On my days off, I often had coffee (called elevenzees) with their wives.

Londonderry is a town set on a hill on the banks of the river Foyle and is quite close to the sea. In fact Fahan is a beautiful sea side only 5-6 miles from the town and we often visited this place during the week ends. The modern city of Londonderry preserves the original layout of four main streets from the Diamond harbor to four gateways. The main street Ship quay Street is very steep with many narrow streets running from it. There are many places of interest to visit such as the St. Columbus cathedral and the Guildhall. And there are many parks where Elizabeth, Amit and I often went – it was a very peaceful place to be in. The hospital here was the second biggest in Northern Ireland, next only to the Royal Victoria Hospital at Belfast.

Although everyone congratulated me for securing a job in this excellent training hospital, I was not very happy to join a speciality not well known to me. My first day was a complete disaster and indeed I was so scared that till I superannuated, I never dared leaving sight of patients till they recovered fully from their anesthesia. I was posted in the ENT operation theater with Collette Murray who was just one year senior to me and consultant Dr. Williams. It was a standard practice at this place to post the newcomers to this theatre where a large number of short procedures were performed so that the new residents would learn faster. To my ill luck (or perhaps good luck since I learnt a very important lesson that day) on this particular day a middle aged gentleman was being operated, whose larynx had to be removed because of cancer. During this kind of surgery there is excessive bleeding and therefore many methods are used to reduce it, and one of the methods is lowering of blood pressure. The patient had been put to sleep and was attached to various monitors. A new intravenous drug that had been recently introduced was being used to lower the blood pressure and thus minimize bleeding. There was great excitement and a number of doctors had come to see the surgery as well as the demonstration of this drug; since this kind of major operation was not a routine in smaller hospitals, many ENT doctors wanted to observe it. The anesthesiologist team was busy observing monitors and in the process forgot to keep an eye on the flow of this new drug and as a result the blood pressure kept on falling and patient suffered a cardiac arrest. By the time it was realized, it was too late and the patient could not be revived with any amount of resuscitation. For me, it was the second scary episode of seeing a patient die under anesthesia and also a lesson for life never to leave a patient unattended.

After this traumatic and scary introduction to anesthesiology I remained in ENT theatre for the next two months. The ENT surgeon was a very pleasant person who was from the army and had lived in India for many years. He did not mind if there were delays in starting his cases because of our training. We used to do 7-8 cases of tonsillectomies every day and I, thus, learnt the techniques of putting patients to sleep quickly. There were two senior consultants with whom I was posted - Dr. Williams was the chief anesthesiologist at this hospital, and for nearly a month he taught me the basic essentials of anesthetic care. After a few weeks, he would come at a quarter to nine in the morning, help me induce anesthesia, settle the patient and then disappear leaving me to manage all cases on my own. I remained on tenterhooks till the patients recovered completely, used to get really scared and worried what would happen if case there was some mishap and in my heart of hearts I cursed him for leaving me all alone to manage cases. I always thought that I was neither being trained nor guided properly, and it was later that I came to know that he never left me unattended, and would watch my work from some distance, with strict instructions to the sister in charge to summon him immediately in case of any problem. Had he been sitting with me and spoon feeding me I would, perhaps, have never gained confidence in handling problems and facing difficult situations!!

The other consultant was Dr. Lamb with whom most of the junior doctors wanted to work as he was an excellent teacher; most surgeons preferred him as their anesthesiologist. Dr. Lamb had been trained as a surgeon and passed his fellowship examination of the Royal College of London, but unfortunately developed allergy to latex gloves and therefore could not operate. He then he took up anesthesiology; as a trained surgeon he knew the anesthetic requirements of surgery and it was no wonder that most surgeons liked working with him.

My immediate seniors were Cicely Newman, Collette Murray and Morale Lyon. They were all very friendly and helped me. We last met in 1997 at the Bicentenary celebrations of the Royal Victoria Hospital at Belfast where I was invited to deliver a lecture. Collette was a consultant in Southern Ireland and Morale had become a reputed cardiac anesthesiologist at RVH. It was a coincidence and a real pleasure that Dr. Morale Lyons was chairing the session for my lecture and Collette was sitting next to me.

The only person who was a little odd and unpredictable was a Pakistani doctor named Sinarkar who was an elderly lady and had joined six months before I did. Unfortunately she did not get on well with most of the staff, and she would often come to my theatre and start interfering in whatever I was doing, telling me how to fill up syringes and how to inject drugs; perhaps in her own way she wished to help a fellow Asian without realizing that she was getting on my nerves. The sister in charge of theatre did not see eye to eye with her. One particular episode which happened in front of my eyes is engraved in my memory even today. Unlike present day disposable items, we had to use glass syringes for injections. If any were broken we had to sign a form for replacement, giving reasons for breakage. In one particular week Dr. S broke more than 10 syringes, and when she asked for another replacement of the eleventh one, the sister in charge of the theatre became very annoyed. She came to the theatre to confront Dr. S and asked her "how on earth you are breaking so many syringes doctor?" Dr. S picked up a fifty cc syringe from the anesthetic trolley, dropped it on the floor and said "like this sister"!! We were all taken aback; sister was disgusted, could say nothing and walked out of theatre quietly.

Over time, I became proficient in handling day today surgical cases. We often had to go to the psychiatric hospital to provide anesthesia for patients requiring electro convulsive therapy; sometimes help was required for dental cases, especially in small children. Once a patient of head injury was brought to the hospital but as we did not have a neurosurgical unit he had to be transferred to Belfast, so a Royal air force helicopter was hired which landed on the hospital compound near our flats. Cicely and Collette accompanied the patient to Belfast, and the event caused a lot of excitement and we all took many photographs of the helicopter at the hospital grounds.

The surgeons were also very good. I remember two surgeons in particular - Mr. Larry who was very fast, pleasant and a very skilled surgeon and Mr. Piper, a slow and complaining person who had a problem with about almost everything, right from the weather to surgery to anesthesia and anything he could think of. There were two operating sessions, the first from 9 am to 1 pm, and the other from 2 to 5pm. Mr. P. would start his cases at 2 pm and sometimes would operate till 8 pm. We were also not allowed to hand over cases to the emergency team and had to wait till the patients had regained consciousness which meant a delayed exit from the hospital, therefore seniors were not keen to work with him and most of the workload fell upon the juniors.

We had a very pleasant stay at Altanagelvin hospital. On our days off we visited many places or went for picnics with friends. By this time a few other Indian friends had also joined at nearby hospitals and on our weekends we all used to gather at various friends' houses by turn. Fahan, a beautiful sea side near Londonderry was only five miles away, (pronounced as fawn) it is a small town in county Donegal (Eire). It means green field and is named after its patron saint. The place is famous for the grave of Sister Agnes Jones who was trained and worked with Florence Nightingale. Another place of interest nearby was the Giants Causeway which is a natural landscape of cliffs made of polygonal basalt columns in perfect shape and lies along the sea coast on the edge of Antrim plateau. It is made of 40000 massive black Basalt columns jutting out of the sea, perhaps caused by volcanic activity many million years ago. Many legends of giants striding over to Scotland are associated with it and the popular one is that of two enemy giants from Fin mc cool and Fin Mc cay from Ireland and Scotland. This was another place we loved visiting and always took our visitors along.

The ultimate aim of most of the resident doctors working at Altnagelvin hospital was to move to the prestigious Royal Victoria Hospital (RVH) at Belfast which was the only teaching hospital attached to Queen's University or to one of the hospitals affiliated to it. My one year term in anesthesiology was over by the end of July 65 and my husband and I were also keen to move to RVH, even though we both had received extension of our jobs at Derry (Londonderry). We were very fortunate to get extremely good recommendations from our bosses and were able to secure jobs at RVH where we and started working in August.

CHAPTER 9

Belfast is the capital of Northern Ireland. It is a sea port situated at the entrance of river Lgan and is well connected by sea or air to various cities in UK. It is a very picturesque place and there are many places worth visiting in and around the city. The ship titanic was built here, and it has been a centre for Irish linen, and is well known for arts, business and law. It is the main educational hub of Ireland, and the Queens University, Presbyterian and Methodist Colleges, Royal Institute and technical colleges are very well known.

The Royal Victoria Hospital or RVH as it is known, is an internationally renowned centre of excellence, well known for its trauma centre. RVH had its origin in 1872 in a dispensary at Clifton Street which provided only outpatient care. Later a fever hospital was opened at Factory Row which was too small to take care of the large number of patients who flocked to this hospital, and so, funds were raised to build a four story hospital called Belfast General Hospital. As the hospital grew, its exceptional services were duly recognized and in1875, it was renamed Royal Victoria Hospital in the name of the then Monarch, Queen Victoria. It now is Northern Ireland's biggest and best hospital complex linked to four major hospitals.

The Head of the department of Anesthesiology, Prof. JW Dundee was a world-renowned anesthesiologist and it was an honor to work with him. Fortunately for me, he took an instant liking for my work, and made it a point to take me along with him to all his OT's. In addition, he gave me independent charge of few sessions in ENT theatres which were a little away from the main block. He was an excellent teacher, and many years later, when I was a faculty member at PGI Chandigarh, he visited us many times and I had many occasions to interact with him. The other person with whom I was worked was Dr. James Moore who was a well-known expert of local and epidural anesthesia and I learnt all these techniques from him. Dr. Moore was not only an expert and excellent teacher, but also a thorough gentleman. My main postings were in general surgery and ENT, and the working atmosphere was very pleasant and I never felt like an outsider. Eleven o'clock was coffee time and most of the surgeons tried to finish the first few cases by that time when sumptuous snacks were provided for which a nominal amount was deducted from our salaries. I understand that all this is now stopped and one has to pay for any snacks that you wish to have!!

We had rented a flat at a place called Rathcool, and Elizabeth had moved in with us to Belfast and was now with us full time; she would go home only on some weekends. She looked after Amit like her own child and was very fond of him. Unfortunately I lost contact with her after coming to India, and despite many efforts to trace her, we could not get in touch. I really and truly am indebted to her for managing Amit and our house with full dedication. Amit also started going to a play school for two hours and enjoyed it tremendously. Usually, the school did not admit children below the age of two and a half years, but he was a very talkative child and the school headmistress was so impressed by him that she took him in immediately. By now the frequency of his chest infections had also become negligible and we had started enjoying a comfortable routine

Though we were quite well settled in Belfast, I still could not adjust to the speciality of anesthesiology. To my young mind it was a speciality of anonymity and I wanted to be amongst people who were awake and with whom I could interact. In anesthesiology one went inside the OT in the morning came out in the evening. For patients you were masked people without any identity, and no matter how hard you worked to save any one or to give best of conditions to the surgeons to operate, the ultimate credit was that of the surgeon alone. Fortunately in the last few decades, things have started changing, and surgeons as well as general public have realized the importance of anesthesiology and the importance of a good anesthesiologist.

The working hours for an anesthesiologist generally were very long; one could not leave patients till they had fully recovered, hence there was no fixed time when I would reach home. Invariably by the time I reached home Amit was asleep and when I left home in the morning he was still sleeping. I, therefore, was quite miserable and wanted to go back to medicine once again and talked to Prof. Dundee about my plight. He tried to convince me to stay back and also promised to make sure that he would teach me so well that I would get through the fellowship examinations. His exact words were "I will see to it that you get the fellowship" but I was adamant and in spite of his repeated advice, I decided to leave RVH. Prof. Dundee was a thorough gentleman, and when he realized that it was futile to convince me and that I was extremely unhappy in the speciality, he let me leave. He did not take any offence at my leaving in the middle of the session; on the contrary, he fixed a job for me in chest medicine at White Abbey Hospital in Belfast.

I took an instant liking for White Abbey hospital as did my boss to me. The nursing staff of the ward was extremely pleasant and we all worked as a family. The sister in charge of the ward was Sister Tolerton, a very pleasant, efficient and able administrator. She was gentle, always smiling and had a very positive approach towards all. She became very fond of me and took more than adequate care of me. Staff Nurse Robb was another who became very friendly with me. She had been recently widowed and, as told by all, had withdrawn from any social activities and did not talk to even her closest friends. It was a surprise for the ward staff that she became so friendly with me that she poured out her heart to me. She even took me to her home and talked about her recently deceased husband about whom she did not wish to talk to anyone else; she had torn all his photographs except one which she showed to me.

If the working conditions are favourable, if your work is appreciated then the whole atmosphere at the work place as well as at home becomes pleasant and that is what was happening to us both. I was now very happy working in the speciality that I liked so much, and was able to see a number of interesting cases and was gaining good experience. Sister Tolerton, nurse in charge of our ward, and her staff made me feel very secure and looked after me extremely well. If ever I was called for an emergency at night they would never let me leave without having a cup of coffee, and if I was called to see a patient in the middle of night nurses would not let me drive home without taking a bowl of soup and hot buttered toast. Satti, my husband was also getting plenty of surgical experience, and his boss Mr. Kemp was another very pleasant person who was very popular amongst his colleagues and patients alike. Satti also had enough spare time to prepare for his FRCS primary examination which he soon cleared, and we decided to move to England where he had secured a registrar's job at Sheffield Infirmary.

Our stay of one year at white abbey hospital had been very pleasant and enjoyable. My ward staff was very sad on learning that we were to leave for England, and a few days before we left, Sister Tolerton, along with the local town people, arranged for a big mass and tea party at the White Abbey Church to pray and wish me and my husband good luck and success. We were both overwhelmed at such an extraordinary gesture and we both felt sorry to leave, but then, parting is a reality and a part of life. And sometimes for moving ahead one has to break away from old ties.

Before taking up our respective jobs we decided to visit India as we had not met our people for more than four years. After spending two months in India with our respective families in 1966 we returned to UK to pursue our careers. By this time I had been offered a registrars job in anesthesiology in Doncaster Royal Infirmary courtesy Prof Dundee, who, for reasons unknown to me, was very keen that I should continue working in anesthesiology (I do not know why?). Jobs in Medicine were few and since this was a registrars post with more money, all our friends advised me to take up the job. Thus I moved to Doncaster and my husband to Sheffield in England.

Chapter 10

Doncaster is an historic market town situated in the north of England that was founded on the river Don by the Romans due to its strategic position on transport and easy connectivity. The town of Doncaster sits at the heart of a vast metropolitan area and has open green spaces, nature reserves and a variety of fauna and flora and with a rich horse racing and railway heritage. Doncaster Royal Infirmary (DRI), started as a dispensary in 1792, is now a key hospital in the region. It was considered a very busy hospital at that time, and as it was situated on the outskirts of the busy London motorway, almost every day cases of serious vehicular accidents were admitted to the hospital. The emergency services were extremely well organized, the blood bank remained open 24 hours and anesthesiology and surgical services were available instantly. Apart from accidents, the hospital also catered to the obstetric service for a very large area. My boss Dr. HB Young was an old man (no pun intended).

Since there were only two registrars we had to be on call on alternate days and even after working the whole night we had to do the routine lists as well till five in the evening. This meant that we were on our feet for nearly 36 hours continuously. I was also on call every alternate week end. The week end started on Friday evenings and finished on Monday mornings. Unfortunately for me my routine list on Mondays started at 9 am and was over at 5. In addition Monday was again my call day. I was free only on Tuesday evenings after my routine list. This meant that including the week end duties and the routine lists I was working for over 72 hours from

Friday to Tuesday evenings. The whole working system in UK has now changed and no one works for more than forty hours in a week, but our times were different, the doctors were considered a dedicated lot who were not expected to complain and raise their voice against the duty hours or the administrators.

The other registrar belonged to Calcutta (now known as Kolkata), but somehow, Dr. Young was quite unhappy with her. She had been trained in India and he always felt that her training was not adequate because she was unable to handle even very simple and uncomplicated surgical cases. As for me, Dr. Young always wanted me in his theatre and would often disappear to do his private cases at nearby private nursing homes, leaving me all alone to manage the morning lists and then would appear later with a cheque for me in his hand as a gift for standing in for him. He always made it a point to call me out for a cup of tea, signaling me to come out by making a T with his fingers. One of our surgeons, Mr. Aikin was a terror in the operation theatres; he was an excellent surgeon, very particular about sterility inside the operating area and would even cut the hairs of nurses and doctors if he saw even a strand of hair coming out of their theatre caps. It was a great surprise for the theatre staff that Mr. Aikin was always complimenting me for my anesthetic management. He would often say "I wish you were not married, I would have taken you out on a date", and even invited me to see a movie once, which I declined and he was genuinely sorry.

As there was shortage of senior house officers at the hospital Dr. Young gave appointment to my friend Anuradha on my recommendation. The hospital had provided me a fully furnished three bedroom flat and since I was alone, we both shared the same accommodation and hired another maid named Sandra to look after her daughter and Amit. By this time Elizabeth who had moved with me to England had gone back to her mother as she was missing her and also was not very keen to take the responsibility of looking after two children.

My husband was working at Sheffield; we could visit each other only occasionally. I had a Fiat 800, and on weekends I drove the car to Sheffield along with Amit, and it was indeed a pleasure to drive on the motorway where there were neither rickshaws, cows, three wheelers, horses, donkeys or dogs.

Dr. Young was quite happy with Anuradha's work as well and she was quickly picking up anesthesiology techniques; unfortunately for her she realized that she was expecting her second child and therefore decided to go back to Belfast, where her husband was already working. We have remained in contact with each other's families even after more than forty years, have lived in the same town in India as well for over thirty years now and meet often. Our children too, have carried this friendship into the next generation, and it gives me great pleasure to see us all still together as a family.

Working at Doncaster was extremely tiring and I had very little time me or my family. My boss was very nice to me; he gave me sucha nice testimonial when I left and I still treasure it. I do not remember much about other consultants except Dr. Sheppard and Dr. Kinish. Dr. Kinish was a clinical assistant and always second on call with me but not very keen on attending emergency calls. Once I was doing a cesarean section at the obstetric hospital which was about 6 km from the main hospital and one of the surgeons wanted to operate urgently on a patient of intestinal obstruction at the infirmary. I could not leave the patient who was already undergoing a cesarean section so I requested Dr. Kinish to start this particular case of intestinal obstruction. He flatly refused to do so even though he was on call. The patient's condition was fast deteriorating but the surgeon had to wait till I was free, and gave Dr. Young his feedback. Dr. Young gave Kinish a piece of his mind the very next day after which he very sheepishly apologized to me.

In June 1967 we decided to take a trip to Europe. One was allowed a holiday of 6 weeks in one year while working in any hospital, and we decided to take four weeks off to see Europe. One could either take a conducted tour with a travel company or make one's own arrangements, and we decided to be on our own so that we could see places we were interested in at our own leisure that, and not at the mercy of the tour operators. We booked various flights and hotels and went to France, Holland, Germany, Belgium, Spain, Denmark, Switzerland and Italy, really enjoying the time, until one night, in Holland, Amit started having severe cough and wheezing. We were so scared that we cut short our holiday and returned to England next day.

The specialist at Doncaster advised us to get Amit's tonsils removed, which was done a few days later. But from that time Amit started having repeated attacks of asthma. It is the children only who can give stress of all kinds to their parents all their lives - whatever illnesses Amit had, they were always in their severest form. Once he contracted measles and developed encephalopathy. When he had mumps, he had all possible complications. I am sure most of the mothers can imagine the stress and mental agony I have gone through !!

As I have already mentioned earlier, Doncaster Royal was one of the busiest hospitals on the motorway and I had little time to look after Amit who was getting repeated attacks of asthma and needed constant care. Luckily, I was able to get a locum consultant post at a town called Boston. This was an indefinite locum and I could work here as long as I wished. At the same time my husband, who had cleared his FRCS, was also offered a senior registrars post so we decide to join this place and by 1967 we were well settled at London Road Hospital in Boston, UK.

Boston is a small town near the east coast of Lincolnshire. It is a historic and an attractive market town known for its 14th century Botolph church that has a high, almost 270 feet tower that can be seen from miles around. The town is 120 miles from London, and like any other English town, is self-sufficient; there was also a corner shop near the hospital where we could run down to for our daily needs. Skegness, a beautiful sea side, is situated nearby with a 6 mile long beach and is a well-known holiday resort.

We were allotted a three bed roomed fully furnished, lovely bungalow within the hospital campus. Amit was nearly four and had started going to school and we now were well settled. The hospital was not very busy and thus after many years, for the first time we were together as a family and were beginning to enjoy our stay in UK. Dr. Kulkarni, our friend from Omagh had also moved to Lincoln, a nearby town, and had joined general practice. I often stood in for him and looked after his practice whenever he was away to India on his holidays. We visited each other often and enjoyed going to Skegness often during free weekends. Many of our classmates and friends also had, by now, come to UK and were working at nearby hospitals, and over the weekends we would gather at someone's house by turn and spend time together. Our very dear friend Dr. RK Tandon had also come to England, and he stayed with us for a while, later settling in UK and becoming a well-known eye surgeon. The nearby town of Spalding was famous for its tulips and daffodils, and every year had a beautiful flower parade which we often visited.

There was plenty of surgical work for my husband. His boss Mr. Pilcher was very happy with him and was letting him do all major cases independently. I was also now a consultant and quite happy with work, and also had plenty of time to relax. But our parents were not happy and felt that since we had both done our postgraduation, there was no need for us to stay in a foreign land. Every fortnight there was a letter from my father-in-law beseeching us to come back to India, and in 1968 we decided to come back to due to constant pressure from family, although my husband had been offered a Clinical Assistant post at the reputed Guy's Hospital in London.

PART 3

PGI, JIPMER AND PGI AGAIN!

CHAPTER 11

Chandigarh is a union territory in north India and serves as a capital of the states of Panjab and Haryana. As a union territory, the city is directly ruled by the union government. This city was the first planned city post-independence and is known world over for its architecture - the name Chandigarh was given after the ancient temple of Hindu goddess Chandi Devi.

One of my maternal uncles had heard a lot about the Postgraduate Institute (PGI) Chandigarh which was at that time talked about as a premier medical institute of the country. He was after us to contact the place, ad since we had neither any job in the country nor a Godfather; we decided to visit PGI before deciding to apply. Transport to the city in late sixties was not very good, and one night in April we boarded the Kalka mail, the only train available, from Delhi at midnight and reached Chandigarh around 4 in the morning. The railway station was just a two roomed block and looked like a dilapidated village station. Had we not requested the coach attendant to let us know when the train arrived in Chandigarh, and had he not woken us up, we would have missed the station! There were no taxis, buses or three wheelers, and so, we were forced to stay in a stinking waiting room till it was daylight, when we took a rickshaw to the town. The rickshaw wala took us to the only reasonable hotel in the city, called Aroma, which too, was not up to the mark. There was no air conditioning, and only a room cooler, which too, functioned at its own will. The first impression of the town therefore was not too good.

The building of PGI was impressive, with greenery all around and lovely flowering Gulmohar trees. We met the then Director Dr. Santokh Singh Anand in his office at the ground floor. He spoke very highly of his institute, particularly of his department of surgery (of which he was also the head) but showed his inability to offer us faculty positions because, first of all there were no vacancies, secondly according to him we "had had no experience of working in India" (Although, a few years later Dr. Anand's own son was given a senior faculty position without having worked in India!!!). It sounded like something which is told to Indian doctors in UK - our friend Dr. Malhotra who had done his MRCP within three months of arriving in UK was told that he was too qualified for a houseman's job and not experienced enough to get a registrar's post. However, Dr. Anand promised to offer us faculty positions as soon as they were available, and he also advised me to register for MD degree of Punjab University and asked us both to join as registrars in our respective departments. We had no idea as to what a registrar was since we had left the country as students and had come back after nearly seven years. In UK,a registrar's post was a senior and respectable post and was generally given only after doing post graduation, and we had no idea that this was not the case in our own country. We were offered the post of registrars, although, later, we saw people with similar qualification being given faculty positions only because either they were related to senior hospital administrators or were children of their doctor friends.

I think my husband must be the only surgeon who became a registrar in India after obtaining FRCS which was a highly rated and coveted qualification recognized world over. The other person I have been told was perhaps Dr. HN Khattri who was also made to a join as registrar in medicine at the PGI, despite having obtained his MRCP, another world recognized degree. Although it was said that PGI attracted faculty from all over India, most of them had been drawn from one particular college in the region, perhaps because most them were students of senior faculty and well known to them. This was our first introduction to discrimination, that too, in our own country. We also met Dr. HS Sachdeva, a senior professor in Surgery who was very keen that we should join the place. He took an instant liking to both of us and always treated us like his family members. Unfortunately he passed away due to a massive heart attack a few years later.

We joined PGI as registrars in May. I also appeared for the MD examination of Panjab University, and was the only candidate out of four who was able to clear the examination. True to his promises, the Director offered me the post of lecturer in my specialty in 1969 but I declined it as there was nothing for my husband.

After joining as a registrar I realized that department of anesthesiology was the most neglected one at this prestigious premier institute. The head of the anesthesiology was not an anesthesiologist but a surgeon, and the senior most in anesthesiology was an elderly gentleman named Dr. Chanan Singh. There was no professor in the specialty, and since Dr. Singh was only a diploma holder and did not possess an MD degree in anesthesiology he could not be appointed as the professor. All the other faculty members were also diploma holders, but later, three of them passed MD examination in anesthesiology. Dr. Chanan Singh was a simple man and was dominated by surgeons, to the extent that I sometimes felt that he was treated as a slave of the surgical departments. Although he was an elderly man, surgeons did not seem to show any respect towards him. I found it very strange to see that quite often he would go off to sleep while sitting on a stool while surgery was going on, and sometimes there were mishaps; perhaps this was the reason for his not being given due respect.

There were four other faculty members in the department - Dr. Harivir Singh, Dr. YS Varma, Dr. BR Mittal and Dr. (Mrs.) GK Singh. On my first day in the operation theatre the first person I was introduced to was Dr. GK Singh and the welcome sentence she uttered was "why did you join this wretched place?" We became fast friends over time, and she looked after me like family. It was only many years later that I realized the wisdom of her words.

Hospital work started at 8 am and was over by 5 pm. There were eight operating theatres on the fourth floor of the building, and in addition, all kinds of emergencies were accepted and operated in the emergency OT on the second floor. Since no office space had been allotted to the department of anesthesiology, we usually sat in the coffee room in the main operating theatre till it was time to go home. There was no place for classes to be held and there were hardly any teaching sessions. If at all any academic activity was held, it would be in one of the vacant rooms in the medicine block on the fourth floor.

There were only two more registrars at that time, Phoola Kaul and Chakravorty. Since the number of was limited, quite often surgeons, in emergency, had to wait for their turn to operate. This created problems for the anesthesiologist on emergency duty. Often there were arguments amongst surgeons and anesthesiologists as to which patient should be operated first and the anesthesiologists were generally made the scapegoat for any delays. Since we were only three registrars in anesthesiology, we had to be on duty every third day, and we remained busy throughout the twenty four hours duty. Dr. IM Bali, who had done his post graduation in surgery but then switched to anesthesiology, joined us after a few months, which gave us all some relief. Dr. Bali and our family took an instant liking for each other and we have remained friends all our lives.

For the first few days after I joined I was made to rotate to various operating theatres (OTs) and observe their working. The OTs were not well equipped, and although the methods of putting the patients to sleep at PGI were also same as in England, most of the work was done manually since there were hardly any machines available. My first day with Dr. Mittal in plastic surgery theatre is worth a mention. He wanted to show me some special techniques of endotracheal intubation. Here I would like to explain as to what endotracheal intubation is - anesthesiologists, during surgery, prefer to paralyze the patient by giving certain drugs. When the patient is paralyzed he/she cannot breath therefore artificial respiration has to be instituted. For this purpose a tube called endotracheal tube is passed in the trachea (wind pipe) and the patient then is connected to machines for providing artificial respiration. Dr. Mittal wanted me to pass the endotracheal tube without using a Laryngoscope, a special instrument, which helps in visualizing the respiratory passages. Since this particular patient had a wide gap in his cheek (part of his cheek had been removed because of cancer during previous surgery) he wanted to pull the tongue forward with the help of a special forceps called Magill forceps so that I could visualize the trachea where the tube had to be inserted. He put the patient to sleep, paralyzed him and pulled the tongue out, but unfortunately for him and also for the patient instead of the forceps, in his hurry he picked up a pair of scissors and while pulling the tongue split it into two from the middle! It now resembled a snake's tongue, and he was in jitters. The plastic surgeon was mad with rage, to the extent that I began to wonder whether they would start hitting each other. Finally, the surgeon Dr. CP Sawhney cooled down, and had to repair the tongue first before proceeding to repair the cheek. This was an extraordinary introduction to anesthesia at PGI for me!!

Dr. (Mrs.) GK Singh and I were the only two persons who had been trained in U.K. therefore surgeons thought highly of us and we were in great demand. In fact once when an emergency cesarean operation for the wife of one of the senior surgeons was to be done, he personally came home to take both of us to the hospital. Since the patient was a VIP (wife of a senior faculty member), we were surrounded by all the senior staff (including the Director of the Institute),which did give both of us a trying time but all was well in the end and the patient came out of anesthesia without any complications!

The department of anesthesiology had only 7-8 total members and we got on well with each other. We often had potluck parties at various houses and also went for picnics together. It was only later when the number of faculty increased that infighting and bickering between various members started because of competitive feelings, jealousies and one-upmanship, however it was a shame that, in this well recognized tertiary care institute the department of anesthesiology, which is one of the most important departments, did not have a professorial chair, and indeed it was painful to see that it was headed by a surgeon.

CHAPTER 12

Life was not easy on the home front. I was expecting my second child, and there was hardly any help available. We often had guests at home since my husband's large family was very keen to see how the "England returned" couple were adjusting to life. For one's daily needs one had to stand in queues to get monthly ration. Sugar, flour, pulses were not freely available and so was the problem with cooking gas. In England we were used to picking up our groceries from shops, there were all kind of gadgets at home and no shortage of any item. But here, in India, even if one had money one could not purchase as few essential items due to paucity, restrictions or non-availability. There were frequent electricity failures, so even if you had gadgets for cooking or cleaning, you could not use them. Once we had 22 guests at home and had to borrow beds beddings etc. from friends. My mother in law and I were spending our whole time in cooking and cleaning etc.

In august of 1968 my younger Robin son was born. He was a chubby healthy child and no bother to anyone, and we employed an ayah to look after him. The hectic work schedule combined with multiple domestic problems, frequent illness of my elder son were all taking a toll of our mental and physical health, and we had almost decided to go back to UK where our jobs were still available.

My father was an upright man and was friend to many bigwigs. The Home Minister of India was closely related to us; the cabinet secretary who later became Governor of Punjab was my father's maternal uncle's son, the chief minister of one state was his close friend and class mate, but he thought it below his dignity to ask for any favors. Although after clearing my MS degree I was offered the post of lecturer at PGI Chandigarh my husband was still not given the promised lecturer post. Therefore without even telling my father, I quietly went to my father's cousin, who at that time was the finance secretary to the government of India, and narrated our tale of our woes to him. I will forever remain indebted to him that he got both of us appointments as lecturers at Jawaharlal Lal Institute of Medical Education and Research (JIPMER), Pondicherry. Suddenly our luck seemed to have changed, and we also received offers from JN Medical College, Aligarh and just when we were about to board the train to Pondicherry, my brother in law brought appointment letters from PGI, Chandigarh offering both of us the post of lecturers. Anyway, the decision was already made, and we arrived at Pondicherry after a forty eight hour train journey with our bag, baggage, children, and Parmanand, our faithful servant who had decided to accompany us to Pondicherry. We were put up at the JIPMER guest house until we got our own accommodation.

Pondicherry town (now known as Pudducherry) is the headquarters of the union territory of Pondicherry. Legends associate this town with sage Agastya who travelled from the Himalayas and settled here. For almost 300 years it was the center of Anglo-French conflicts, and later became the retreat of freedom fighters as well as Shree Aurobindo. Pondicherry, popularly called as Pondy became a French colony in 1665 and remained so till 1954, and even at that time, retained its French character. Neat, pleasant and charming, the city has a beautiful beach and a refreshing sea side with lovely houses built along the coast line.

JIMPER is one of the outstanding medical institutions in India. At that time, it was a 600 bed teaching hospital with a beautiful campus and lovely, evergreen parks with beautiful statues. The main building was three storied, the walls of which were decorated with large murals, some depicting ancient Indian medical history. It traces its origin to 1823 when a medical school called "Ecole de medicine de Pondicherry" was started by the French and later taken over in 1956 by the government of India.

The department of anesthesiology at that time was small and headed by Prof. NP Singh, a dynamic personality who forever was ready to fight for his department and its members. The other members were Drs. Chakraborty, Prem Budhiraja and Saunderajan. There were few junior doctors also, one of them, Dr. Gopal Rao, always had some interesting anecdotes to narrate but did not get on well with our Professor and later took up Gynecology as his specialty. Dr. Saunderajan, though on a junior post, was an elderly lady and we all respected her. She was a Christian married to a Hindu. Her husband was a senior retired wing commander from Indian Air Force and it was a pleasure to see how their family celebrated all Hindu and Christian festivals. They were a perfect example of communal harmony and I am proud to say that we became fast friends and often had dinners and also went on various holidays together. It was great to see that Dr. Saunderajan always called a spade a spade and did not spare even the head of the department; perhaps it was easy for her due to her being much older in age to Dr. Singh.

On the first day I met our head, Prof. NP Singh, he gave me the task of making an anesthesia chart for the hospital. It took me nearly a week to complete it, but it turned out to be comprehensive, with two full pages of pre- and post-operative information. Dr. N.P Singh was extremely happy to see it, and it was instantly accepted and printed for use; perhaps it still is being used. During each surgery, the anesthesia chart had to be filled up in duplicate using carbon paper - one copy was attached to the patient file and the other was kept in the department for use in writing scientific papers and also in case of any dispute from either the surgical departments or from patients.

Prof. NP Singh had an admirable personality though many surgeons did not get on well with him; I must admit that I did pick up few good habits from him. He was very punctual and would be inside the operating room, all changed and gowned before anyone else and surgery would start at eight am daily. The operation theatres were on three floors, at each floor there was a twin complex of operating theatres, and Dr. Singh had to go up and down few times to check if everything was running smoothly. Two junior and one senior person were always posted at each complex. In each OT one register had to be filled daily with details of anesthesia and surgery and the time it took for a particular person to perform surgery. No cases were cancelled, and any surgery which went beyond 2 pm had to be entered in red in the register. The purpose of all this was to ensure that all cases were over in time so that the operating theaters were cleaned and sanitized for the next day's list and also to keep a check on the surgeons so that they did not overburden the staff. He also started a pre anesthesia clinic where all cases were seen and investigated before surgery. Patients who were cleared at this clinic could not be refused surgery. For the first few days I was just made to rotate to various operation theaters and observe the working in the theatres. The O.T's were not very well equipped and there were hardly any ventilators or monitors available. The patient's parameters had to be monitored manually by the feel of pulse, color, respiration, blood pressure etc.

Like Prof. NP Singh, Dr. Makhani, who was the head of Orthopedics was another person who was ready with his knife at 8 am and could not tolerate a delay of even five ten minutes; however it was a pleasure to work with him. Between 8 am and 1 pm he would operate on an average of 12-13 major and minor cases. He was very appreciative of my work but as far as punctuality was concerned he did not spare any one. I lived a little distance away from the hospital at a place called Elangonagar, and once, due to heavy traffic I could not reach hospital in time and Dr. Makhani's list was delayed for 15 minutes. Although he did not say anything to me and was very pleasant all day, he did complain to Prof. N.P. Singh in writing regarding his list starting 15 minutes late!!

Many surgeons did not see eye to eye with Prof. N.P. Singh and there were always some arguments. Prof. Singh was obstinate quite often and did not listen to anyone. One great quality of this man was that he would never insult or scold his juniors in front of any other department faculty even if the person had committed blunders but would always side with them; later he would call the erring person to his office and literally skin him/her. In an emergency he would go out of his way to help anyone, and I can never forget the day when my brother in law's colleague was involved in a road traffic accident in Delhi and Prof. NP Singh even donated his own blood to save him. I remained in contact with him till he passed away a few years ago, and I pray to God to rest his soul in peace.

During that time, Professor Sporel from Ontario, Canada, came to JIPMER for six months and brought with him many new techniques. We took full advantage of learning from him and his experiences and teachings. One of his techniques called "transtracheal jet ventilation" became very popular later all over the world and we all felt proud to have worked and known, such a renowned anesthesiologist so closely.

There were no super specialties in JIMPER and we did not handle major cardiac or neurosurgical cases, though some minor cardiac surgery was often done by Prof. Naraynan who had a terrible temper inside the OT but was a very pleasant man outside! All in all, JIMPER was a friendly place, and with limited faculty members in various department, everyone helped and cared for each other.

Our elder son Amit was almost eight years old. He had gotten admission to the central school on the campus, and although we lived a little distance away at Elagonagar, it was easier for us to bring him with us to the campus. Robin our younger son stayed at home with Parmanand (our servant) and an ayah whom we had employed after joining at JIMPER. After school, Amit stayed with Dr. and Mrs. Rastogi in the campus till we finished our work at the hospital. Dr. Rastogi was a senior scientist with the Hospital; they were an elderly couple and very helpful. Mrs Rastogi looked after Amit very caringly, and even their grown up children became very fond of Amit. Robin, though not even 2, got admission to a well-known school called St. Cloony's, in town, where he also was very happy. We loved being at Pondicherry and often visited the sea side which was not far away from the institute. Only problems which bothered us was that our jobs were ad hoc i.e. temporary and as when the regular employees joined we would have to leave the place, but thanks to the Almighty that my husband soon was made regular through UPSC and my appointment soon followed.

The town of Pondy has famous for the Sri Aurobindo Ashram and Mother. A township named Auroville was also established nearby where people from all over the world congregate. It had a huge urn which contains earth from all over the world indicating universal brotherhood.

Sri Aurobindo (August 15, 1872-December 5, 1950) was a great scholar, mystic, poet, yogi and an aggressive Indian nationalist who was actively involved in the politics of India and is well known for his incredible contribution to the freedom struggle of our country. His literary works span a variety of subjects like Indian culture, socio-political aspects and spiritualism. It is said that Sri Aurobindo went into a state of deep meditation for almost four years in Pondicherry; in 1920, his close spiritual collaborator named Mirra Richard who is more popularly known as 'The Mother' joined him and later, the idea of establishing an ashram in Auroville took seed.

The "Mother" was born Mirra Alfassa in Paris on 21 February 1878. In 1914 she came to Pondicherry to meet Sri Aurobindo, whom she immediately recognized as the one who for many years had inwardly guided her spiritual development. After a brief stay, she returned to France only to return in 1920. When the Sri Aurobindo Ashram was formed in 1926, Sri Aurobindo entrusted its full charge to her, and under her guidance for nearly fifty years, the Ashram grew into a large, multi-faceted spiritual community. In 1952 she established Sri Aurobindo International Centre of Education, and in 1968 an international township, Auroville. For anyone visiting Pondicherry it was a must to visit Aurobindo Ashram to get the Mother's blessing. Twice a year, she came to the balcony of the Ashram to give darshan, to the general public. We were lucky to have visited the Ashram many times and received her blessings on many occasions.

Although Pondicherry was a friendly and sociable place, for us the major problem was distance - unlike today, trains moved slowly and it took nearly 3 days between Delhi and Pondicherry. Air services were not only expensive, but few and far between. It took us almost two days to reach my in-laws place and another day to reach Nainital, amounting to a total of eight days wasted in our vacations in just commuting. In case of any illness in the family it was almost impossible to reach them in time. Fortunately, in 1972 we both were offered the post of senior lecturers at PGI Chandigarh, and after deliberating on the pros and cons, we finally decided to move to Chandigarh, the biggest reason in favor of this decision was that we would be much closer to our families and near and dear ones. We sold off all our limited household goods and made the move back to Chandigarh.

We had recently purchased a Fiat car and decided to make the journey by road, an eventful 5 day journey in which our first encounter was with a buffalo who thought it was her right to cross the road first when our car had just picked up speed. The result of this was that the head light of our brand new car was broken and had to be repaired but fortunately no harm came to the thick skinned animal or to any of us. Then there were potholes and ditches that needed to be negotiated carefully; another very strange habit of the owners of the tea shops and farms along the roads was to stand in the middle of the road and gossip with each other, without any care for oncoming traffic – when the drivers honked, they went back to their side of the road!! Every evening, after sun down we stopped at some reasonably priced hotel and also visited various places of interest such as the Ellora caves, Indore and Gwalior fort, Taj Mahal, etc. Once when we reached the city of Shivpuri we could not find any place to stay. Our landlord at Pondicherry was an engineer with the public works department (PWD) and had given us his reference and so we went to PWD rest house. Fortunately the place was vacant and the caretaker knew our landlord and we were accommodated for the night.

The highway known as the national highway number one Or NH-1 was full of pot holes and ditches and our car which was absolutely new had to bear the brunt of it all. Car tires had to be changed frequently; they punctured often due to nails on the roads. Because of extremely bad road conditions our brand new car had started showing signs of wear and tear and once, the axel of the car broke down. This would have been no problem had it happened near a town but the problem arose near the Chambal ravines, a place which was known to be infested with dacoits. No one who passed through was willing to stop; ultimately one truck driver helped us by towing the car to a nearby town and we thanked our lucky stars to have been saved. Had anyone guessed that I was carrying all my gold jewelry with me it would have been disastrous.

CHAPTER 13

After a back breaking adventurous journey on national highway number one we reached Chandigarh safe but tired and reached our close friend Dr. Kak's residence in October 1972 and joined our respective appointments the very next day. Our problem now was to find accommodation in the PGI campus, but since no houses were vacant in the PGI campus, we started looking for a place to stay outside in town, Fortunately for us, a doctor couple, the Chakravartys, were going to London on one year study leave and they let us have their house until they returned. They packed all their household goods into one room and gave us a free run of their huge, four bed roomed house. Both, Amit and younger son Robin got admission into St. John's school, and in addition to Parmanand, we also employed another maid servant Kalawati and the home front was satisfactory.

We always had a spate of guests at home my husband had a reasonably large family with eight siblings, their wives and children. If anyone had a medical problem they always liked to consult at PGI and as a result, we always had someone around. The family was very traditional and had firmly fixed ideas and the daughter in law was duty bound to look after the elders. In my case I was the youngest daughter in law and therefore was expected to take care of anyone who came to our place. Having come from a highly educated, very modern family, it at times was very difficult for me to understand or to accept their way of thinking, but I always made them all feel very welcome. Fortunately even with all their orthodox traditional thinking and superstitious beliefs they were all very loving and always extended a helping hand in managing the household wherever they visited us. My mother in law was the sweetest of them all and very loving and caring towards me. She was not very educated, but she was very well versed in the ways of life, and very witty and always ready with an answer that would make people speechless.

In a male dominated society, a women professional has to work doubly hard to compete and be better or equal to the male members. A married woman in the Indian set up is expected to look after the household, she is no goddess yet she is expected to be like goddess Durga who has many hands and be able to do multiple tasks at one time, also be caring to the whole family i.e. not only to her husband and children but to other family members as well. In this whole process, my professional work of reading, looking up the recent literature would invariably get delayed and it only after 11 or 12 pm could I sit with my books and finish my pending work. Professional work was very heavy, and quite, often during the day I did not get time to come out of the operation theater to even have a meal; there was also a shortage of staff in the department and we had to attend emergencies often in the middle of night. To top it all Amit had developed severe asthma and every ten to fifteen days I had to sit up, with him on my lap, all night because that was the only way he was comfortable and able to breathe. Whenever Amit was down with asthma, I would just visit him to see to his medications, meals etc. and rush back to work without having as much as a cup of tea.

The children were growing up and also needed help in their studies. In Indian schools a lot of homework is assigned to the students. Often the concepts are also not made clear to them, and this was another task which I had to cover. As for my husband, he was quite impatient with children and since I could not tolerate him spanking them, I had to devote time with children, help them in their homework, supervise the kitchen and cater to the needs of the family. In orthodox Indian homes boys are treated as special and thoroughly spoiled by their parents, and my husband was not an exception to this rule. Although a loving husband and a caring father, he had no desire to manage the home front, and in a way we had both divided our tasks - he did all the paper work looked after the financial aspects whereas I cared for our home. Coming from a family where no difference was ever made between girls and boys I found such an attitude very irritating. I had three servants to look after children, for cleaning the house and for cooking, but I had to keep them happy and they were the only reason that I could carry on with my profession. One of them was with me for over forty years and passed away recently due esophageal cancer. My advice to all women professionals is that they should keep their home front well organized and this is the only way one can give full attention to one's profession and succeed.

Since PGI was an academic institute, classes for post graduate students were held every day. In our department, these classes started at 3 pm, and we had to relieve them from all duties so that they could attend. As we did not have adequate staff this meant that we were left on our own to look after the patients in the theaters; at times there were very complicated cases which meant we had to be extremely vigilant all the time and could not them patients unattended. The job of an anesthesiologist is extremely tense as the life of the patient is in their hands and even a slight mistake can cause disaster. The surgical procedures were invariably long and complicated, especially in neurosurgical, renal and pediatric specialties. Some of my surgical colleagues took eight to ten hours in completing the procedures such as anastomosis of vessels in portal hypertension or a renal transplant. Since PGI had a big name in the country, most cases that were referred were complicated and most of the patients suffered from multiple medical problems of other body systems as well; the burden of looking after them fell on the anesthesiologist during, and many times, after surgery.

The anesthetic cover for emergency surgery was provided to the junior doctors of the department by us. We could be called for an emergency any time of day or night and as a rule we had to be present for emergency operations of neonates, neurosurgical and cardiac procedures. The hospital emergency was always busy and we were involved in emergency services round the clock - sometimes there were 26 emergency surgeries in 24 hours including three to four caesareans. Nearly twenty five years back or perhaps more, a study was published in a reputed American anesthetic journal where it was reported that the incidence of heart attack and suicide was highest amongst anesthesiologists. In my own life time I have also come across many cases of heart attack and suicides in my profession, and this is just is one indication of the highly stressful life that we anesthesiologists lead.

In 1973 July the first kidney transplant was done at PGI and I was the first person to have been involved in this very important landmark. The surgeons were Drs. RVS Yadav, BC Bapna (Head of Urology) and IC Pathak (Head of Pediatric Surgery) and Dr. Harivir Singh, our departmental head and I were the two anesthesiologists. It was a hush, hush affair and no one except the team were allowed to enter the theaters, and no one except the head of institute even knew that such a surgery was being done. It was done very secretly, after all the cases had been completed in all other operation theaters, and started after 2 pm in the two urology OTs where the donors as well as recipient were put to sleep. It took nearly seven hours to complete the whole procedure. Although the transplant surgeon claimed he had done many transplants before this one, he did not seem very confident, and I felt that perhaps this was the first time he was doing it independently, but I may be wrong.

The transplant was a success initially, and all the newspapers were full of this great achievement over the next few days, but as usual there was no mention of the anesthesiologists and other members of the team. The usual tendency for surgeons generally is to project themselves as a great achievers little realizing that without anesthesia no surgical feat can ever be achieved. It though is a different matter that the patient did not do too well in the postoperative period, developed severe infection and died few days later. From this humble beginning, I remained involved with kidney transplant till I left PGI in1989, and I was often invited to many fora to deliver lectures on anesthetic problems related to transplantation. As time progressed, our surgeons and anesthesiologists all became experts and many of them who trained at PGI have now spread all over the world.

In 1974, my son Amit had a serve attack of Asthma which could not be controlled with intensive bronchodilator therapy. Fortunately for him, our friend Inder Mohan Bali had just returned from RVH, Ireland after training in Anesthesiology and Intensive Care, and our department had acquired a ventilator only a few weeks before he fell ill seriously. It was his destiny that right equipment and right persons were available at the right time, and he was put on ventilator and with the sincere and continued efforts of pediatrician Dr. Lata Kumar and Inder Mohan Bali, he survived. Doctors from all over PGI came to help, and I simply do not have enough words to praise their efforts and will always remain indebted to them. As long as we were in the hospital with Amit, Sudha Kataria another friend and a very caring person, looked after my younger son Robin's daily needs and schooling, etc. I wonder if the children ever realize what their parents have gone through in bringing them up !

In 1974 the junior doctors went on strike since their demand for shorter working hours, raise in salaries, better working conditions etc. had not been fulfilled by the administration in spite of repeated requests. All the senior faculty members were assigned the duties of junior doctors, and at first we were all very enthusiastic and tried to run the services as smoothly as possible. Negotiations went on between the administration and junior doctors but it came to naught and later when the nurses and technicians also joined hands with resident doctors, the hospital came to a standstill. I do not remember the exact details well enough, but I think that after a fortnight, a compromise was reached between the two sides and hospital work was resumed. A committee, called the Kartar Sigh Commission was set up with the health secretary as its chairperson to look into the matter and it made many recommendations in favor of the resident doctors

CHAPTER 14

In May 1975, my father had an attack of severe chronic bronchitis and passed away after a prolonged illness. This was the first time I realized the sorrow of parting from near and dear ones. My husband and I took care of him during his illness. My father was a very patient man and never complained about anything, and everyone feels that I have all his traits, but I am impatient many a times. One great satisfaction we all had was that my brother, his family, my sister and her family and we were all with him when he passed away, and all of us gave him all possible medical support that was available at that time.

My husband had been offered a British high commission scholarship that year and was allowed study leave by the administration. I too was also able to get one year unpaid leave from PGI, and we thus proceeded to London where he joined at Middlesex Hospital in central London and I joined as a senior registrar in one of the suburban hospitals which provided me a lovely flat in the Wexham Park Hospital complex. It used to take me five minutes to reach the OT complex which had four operation theatres. My seniors were Drs. RD Jack and Fell who soon developed confidence in me and left me to do all difficult cases independently. Some of the surgeons were extremely brilliant - two orthopedic surgeons Mr. Saad and Mr. King always were competing with each other to see who would finish cases earlier. They did a large number of hip replacement cases and it indeed was a pleasure to work with them and with Mr. Arden who had developed the prosthesis for hip replacement surgery.

Amit and Robin both were admitted to the local high school which was a walking distance away from the hospital. Our friend Dr. Kulkarni had given us one of his cars and life was very comfortable. Satyendra used to travel daily for a distance of 45 Kms, but his timings were flexible and he was off duty every weekend. His bosses Mr. LeQuesn and Mr. Hobsley made him register for a PhD of London University. My Consultant Dr. Jack always told me that PhD from London University was extremely difficult and impossible; he himself had registered for it but left it halfway through, and he was pleasantly surprised when Satyendra got his PhD.

After we had completed one year stay at London, we went on a tour of the United States in 1976. The year was the 200th year of their freedom and important places like the White House were open to the public and we were able to see various rooms like the Pink room, Green room, Blue room in the White House. We also toured the FBI headquarters, visited Arlington cemetery, and really enjoyed our trip to the most.

Winding up, my husband stayed back in UK to complete his studies, and the three of us returned to India and me to my routine at PGI. During the summer vacations of 1977 we went to UK where my husband was to complete and submit his PhD thesis at the London University. On our return in the month of August I was shocked to learn that Dr. JS Anand from Bombay had been appointed as the professor and head in our department at PGI. Till then, there had been no post of Professor in Anesthesiology at PGI, and the chair of professor had been hurriedly created, no advertisements were made, no interviews were held and he was appointed by the administration. In this, some faculty members from our department were also involved, and had praised this man to be an exceptional cardiac anesthesiologist and academician. It though is a different matter that he turned out to be in total contrast to the image that had been created by him and for him by others. The intensive care unit was started by our department in 1978, and although all the initial work and planning had been done by Dr. Singh who was also able to convince the administration the suitability of anesthesiology department in managing it. Unfortunately for him Dr. JS Anand was given all the credit for the set up, to add insult to injury.

Dr. Harivir Singh, who till now had been heading the department and Dr. YS Verma, the two senior most faculty members in the department went to court against this appointment. The case lasted for nearly eight months and in the end, the verdict came out in favor of them, the court ruled the appointment illegal. Dr. Singh and I were next door neighbors on campus and fast family friends as well, and Dr. GK Singh and I remained his staunch supporters till the case was over. During his tenure as head a large number of faculty used to come to his house as well wishers, on festivals or otherwise, and it was so surprising to see how human nature changes with circumstance – the same people now, during the pendency of the court case, stopped interacting with Dr. Harivir Singh and started meeting Dr. Anand and some even became his followers. The day the court pronounced judgment in favor of Dr. Singh and Dr. Varma, the same persons were again standing at his door with bouquets and boxes of sweets, sweet talking Dr. Singh. It was surprising that the same people who were Dr. Anand's supporters once again became Dr. Harivir's right hand persons and I was amazed to see not only how quickly people changed their loyalties but even more surprised to see that Dr. Harivir Singh accepted them even though he was aware that they were back stabbers and had harmed him. We were certainly the misfits in this kind of society!

However, the fight was not over, and the Administration was hell bent upon re-appointing Dr. Anand, and advertised for the post so as to appoint him within ten days. The three of us represented to the ministry against this illegality, and even met the then health minister who was convinced and cancelled interview. In the end Dr. Anand had to pack his bags and leave and Dr. H. Singh became professor and head a few months later.

In 1982, the Dhar committee recommendations for time bound promotions of faculty members were implemented. Most of the faculty members at PGI at that time, were stagnating at one position and almost eighty percent had spent ten to twelve years at one level. My husband and I had also completed eleven long years as Assistant Professor and our long due promotion to Associate Professors was very welcome. However, everyone had to go through the normal selection process of interviews and although almost all the Assistant Professors were promoted, there were some who were not so lucky, either they did not have enough scientific papers, or their bosses were biased against them and did not want them to be promoted. In any case, the administration too had its own preferences and some faculty members were promoted ignoring their inadequacies. In my own department, where one of the senior faculty had gone on deputation, instead of the next person, someone else was promoted - it is not that that person was any less deserving, but as a matter of routine it should have been the next person in line. In fact one of my colleagues once told me "Madam do not feel sorry for anyone in this Institute, it runs on the policy of tell us the person and we will tell you the rule."

In 1976 there was yet another strike by the junior doctors. This time enthusiasm that was seen among the faculty during the previous strike was nowhere to be seen. All the patients who did not require special treatment were discharged; however, emergency admission remained open. Faculty members from various departments were put on twelve hourly duties. When the nurses also threatened to go on strike, hospital work came to a standstill. Every morning and evening there would be a meeting with the administration and briefing by them but it came to naught. One interesting aspect of the strike was that meals were provided to the on-duty faculty members by the Institute. Even here, some faculty showed pettiness, by eating meals even though they were not on duty, and then they had the audacity to criticize the dietetics department for not catering to their likes and dislikes, often bringing this up during meetings with the director of the institute. The strike lasted for over two weeks and ended only when the demands of the residents were met with.

CHAPTER 15

It is amazing to see how technological advances have made life much easier for teachers and the taught now. I am reminded of those times when we had no computers, electronic type writers or photo copiers etc. The only facility at the department was an epidiascope which I cannot recall whether it was from the department or kept in one of the lecture theaters. Epidiascopes project a magnified image of opaque object/cards onto a screen, and we had to prepare cards that could be projected onto a screen during lectures and seminars. A few years later came the overhead projectors which were used to display images on the screens and for this; transparent sheets were required which were quite costly. The department did not provide them, and they had to be bought by the student presenter or the moderator teacher. Luckily, the sheets could be used again and again after cleaning with spirit until it became impossible to use them due to overwriting.

It was a herculean task to get slides made – these were required for presentation of our research work or lectures at conferences. First of all, charts had to be hand written in capital letters point wise, and then one had to request the stenographer of the department to type them or the Institute artist to prepare them. The junior faculty members had the last priority and had to wait till the last minute or get them prepared from outside by paying artists in town. Unfortunately we had only one steno in our department and only one manual typewriter, and he often took typing work home and made some money by obliging the junior doctors.

If I remember correctly, the department of Gynecology was the first to acquire an electronic typewriter and typing done on this was bright and clear and slides came out beautifully. It was thanks to the head of Gynecology, who was very friendly to us, that I often got my slides typed in that department. Once typing was done next step was to get slides made from the photography department. Again we were at the mercy of this department - the staff there was overworked as the department had to cater to the whole Institute. Fortunately the senior most person Mr. Kohli was very kind and helpful and my slides were always made well in time. It was so different from today, when once can make slides on a laptop or tablet and carry it around so effortlessly. At that time we had no knowledge of computers, and when a computer centre was opened in the city in late eighties, PGI collaborated with it for training faculty members, again, as per the policy of pick and choose! However till 1989-90 when I left PGI, neither an electronic typewriter nor computer was available in the department and most of us didn't even know how computers operated or even how they looked. It was only when I joined Sanjay Gandhi institute that I came across computers.

CHAPTER 16

In life one comes across all kind of people, good and bad. It is indeed difficult to forget some of them and I would like to mention some of my unforgettable experiences. Once I was quite sick and on leave from the Institute, and one of my students along with his wife came to enquire about my health. He also brought a bouquet of flowers. His manners and etiquette had always been perfect, and he seemed very concerned about my health and promised to come back soon. A few days later he came back again in the morning, and I was really surprised to see him in my house during the time when he should have been working in hospital. He seemed to be in a state of complete mental agony and after a while he started sobbing; in between sobs he informed that his mother had had a heart attack at Hyderabad and it was imperative for him to immediately fly home but he had no money and therefore he wanted me to help him by giving him five thousand rupees as loan. I felt really sorry for him, and I was so moved by his crying that I gave him whatever money I had at home. The mother in me felt so sorry for this man that I forgot that his wife was also a doctor and was earning money as a consultant at a nearby hospital. After all it was extremely important for the poor child to be at home with his mother. A month later when I joined work, I came to know that he had conned many persons at the Institute as well as outside with the same story. Luckily, I did get my money back few months later, but many others faced problems in getting their money back.

Sometimes, junior doctors also bickered. I remember of a particular incident when two junior doctors in one particular department did not see eye to eye and one day while sitting in the OPD they got into an argument that soon escalated into a physical fight. One of them got into such a rage that he bit off the thumb of the other and threw it into the dustbin. Fortunately, plastic surgeons present in the theater were successfully able to reattach the severed thumb.

Occasionally there were arguments between the consultant and residents as well. I remember of a particular incident in my department for some equipment that both wanted to use, the senior for his PhD and the junior for his MD thesis, the arguments lead to a physical fight and lo and behold, soon one was on the top of other, pulling each other's clothes. The pajama of one got torn and he was left only in his colorful undies.

As the numbers of faculty members and resident doctors increased, jealousies and personal likes and dislikes also grew and one upmanship also increased. This was quite evident during statistical meetings where surgical mortalities were discussed. Unfortunately as a general rule, doctors, by and large are always ready to criticize each other, and if something goes wrong, there are many to suggest that the treatment given was not correct or surgery had not been done properly. Although statistical meetings were kept with the aim of learning from mistakes in complicated cases or operative/post-operative deaths, it unfortunately deteriorated into leg pulling session of the consultant concerned. Finally, they learnt to put the blame on anesthesiologists even if the surgeon had committed a blunder!

At that time, in PGI, there were eight operation theatres each, on the fourth and fifth floors, where different specialties operated. I have seen a fair share of awkward situations here, sometimes hilarious and sometimes not so much. Once I had anesthetized an old women of 60 (at that time 60 was old for me!!) for the removal of her intestines for cancer. I had been really careful in making her comfortable and pain free, not only because it was a major surgery but also she was the mother of one of our OT nurses. The surgeon, I wouldn't name him, was operating. He was very fond of teaching his post graduates, and as he proceeded with surgery, he explained each and every step to them and also kept on explaining as to how careful they must be when they were near any artery, vein or a nerve. He said "one must be extremely careful while near the ureter (a tube which takes urine from kidneys to the urinary bladder) because if you cut it then you have had it" and next second I heard him shout "bloody hell" and he threw some instruments on the floor. Lo & behold! The surgeon, while explaining the need for being careful, had himself divided the ureter in two halves! There was now a great commotion in the operating room. Fortunately for the surgeon, and more so for the patient, the chief of Urology was also operating that day and he was immediately contacted, and thanks to him the ureter was repaired. It though, is a different matter that patient had to remain under anesthesia for much longer than expected and had to undergo two surgical procedures on her instead of one.

One day, the head of surgery approached me around one pm and requested me to anaesthetize a patient saying that he would finish within half an hour (surgeons generally give much lower estimated times). Since the case was of a haemorrhoidectomy (piles surgery), I was hoping for it to be over in about half an hour and thus decided to put the patient to sleep with the help of a mask. While using a mask one has to hold it by both hands; however the surgery did not take much long and we were all expecting to be free soon. After completion it was time for bandages to be applied. At that time, a pad would be applied around the anus and fixed in place with a T shaped bandage. Our surgeon was not satisfied and he wanted the nurse to give him a bandage "6 inches wide and 36 inches long".

"But sir we do not have such a bandage" informed the nurse.

"Did I not send you the operating list in advance, you should have arranged for it" said the chief.

When the nurse showed her inability to provide such a bandage, he was furious, and shouted "I don't care how and from where you get it. I want a bandage 6 inches wide and 36 inches long" and sat down on a stool in protest.

"Call the sister in charge of theatres".

So the sister was called and she too showed her inability to get such a bandage, but told him that she could make one for him, to which he agreed. So a sterile white bed sheet was brought and it was cut into a 36 inches long piece. The sister made it into a T bandage and handed it to the surgeon.

"Madam," he said, "I did not ask for a T bandage. I wanted a bandage 6 inches wide and 36 inches long" he insisted angrily.

This went on and on for almost three hours and by now my hands were getting tired. Unfortunately it was a Saturday and none of our resident doctors were around, there was only one OT attendant and none of the nurses was trained in anesthesiology so I had to manage on my own. The sisters looked at each other and they had no clue why our surgeon was insisting on this type of bandage. Finally, Sister Philip, the in charge brought out another sheet cut a bandage 6 inches wide and 36 inches long, handed it over to him and walked out, finally ending the whole drama, but my hands were now numb for I had been holding the mask for almost three hours. There were many junior residents of the department of surgery and nurses present in the theatre that day, and if anyone of them comes across this book I am sure they would recall this.

Surgeons also have a tendency to blame the anesthesiologists for surgical mishaps and for their own inadequacies. A few instances always have always remained in my mind. Once, one surgeon was trying to remove a very large tumor from the abdomen of young man. This tumor was sitting on the aorta, the big artery which supplies blood to all organs of body through its branches. He literally snatched the tumor and along with it a piece of aorta and this was immediately followed by excessive, uncontrolled bleeding and the patient succumbed. Untroubled, he came out of theatre and showed the big tumor to the relatives of the patient and told them that he had successfully removed the tumor but unfortunately the patient had not regained consciousness from anesthesia. One of my colleagues, who was the anesthesiologist was shocked to hear this, and fuming with anger, told the patient's relations what had actually happened. Fortunately for the surgeon the patient's relations were illiterate and very poor and had to accept the will of God!

Once I had anesthetized a woman for autotransplant of the kidney. Auto transplant is done in patients who have very severe, high blood pressure due to narrowing of the renal artery which supplies blood to kidneys. This disease is called renal artery hypertension. Nowdays there are many other ways of treating it, but 25 years ago the only certain way, was removal of the kidney from its normal place, bypassing the diseased segment of the artery and re-transplanting the kidney elsewhere. This patient was the wife of a senior faculty at Panjab University, and everything was going on smoothly, until I detected that the pulse was slipping away. I asked the surgeon as to what was going on and to my dismay was informed, that by mistake he had nicked the aorta. There was sudden severe blood loss, the blood pressure fell, and we almost lost the patient. We pumped up all kinds of fluids into the patient and also whatever blood was available to keep her alive. The heart surgeon was urgently called who easily repaired the blood vessel; however surgery took much longer than expected. To my disgust when the surgeon came out, he told the relations that the delay in patient's recovery was due to her taking longer than expected in recovering from anesthesia!!

Our head of the department, too, had his idiosyncrasies. He was totally averse to any one applying for leave, and many times the residents disappeared without taking leave or even informing him; this sometime led to hilarious and odd situation. Once, one of my senior colleagues was running high temperature, and since she did not wish work to suffer, she came to the operation theatre. However, as she was unable even to stand she went to him with her leave application which he immediately tore and said "nope no leave". My colleague was so disgusted that she vowed never to personally give leave application that day onwards. There are many instances of him refusing leave to doctors. Once, two residents were to be married, and went to him with a wedding invitation as well as leave application. He sanctioned their leaves but on separate dates which were nowhere near the wedding date!

In another instance a resident went to him with a wedding invitation and leave application. Leave was refused and he was advised to postpone the wedding for some other day. When he expressed his inability to do so, he was thrown out of the office. Upset, he came to me for advice whether he should disappear, and he did. Surprisingly, our head did not even notice his absence.

Sometimes he was unpredictable and would flare up for no obvious reason. Once he slapped an OT attendant and all OT technicians and attendants went on protest demanding a written apology from him and refused to come inside the operating room. I was witness of the slapping but fortunately for me I had joined only recently and was in OT gown, mask and cap, and no one could identify me and I spared the ordeal of giving evidence. Another time, threw a glucose bottle on an OT technician because he could hang it properly on the drip stand; fortunately the bottle fell on the floor and no harm came to the technician. On another occasion he nearly slapped an ENT surgeon for not controlling the blood pressure of the patient before bringing him to the OT. However, even with all these idiosyncrasies and eccentricities, our boss was a pleasant, simple and mild man, and I often felt that he was too simple and people took advantage of this fact. He passed away few years back due to cancer; May God rest his soul in peace.

The next senior faculty was Dr.YS Varma for whom I have tremendous respect. He was one a great teacher, academician and above all, a very nice man who never got involved in any kind of Institute politics. He never talked ill to anyone and even if narrated your woes to him he would tell you to forget and forgive. The biggest compliment from him to me was when his wife was to undergo hysterectomy, he requested me to anaesthetize her: when his doctor son had a nasal fracture he again requested me to give anesthesia. For me, this was the greatest compliment from a senior, trusting their loved ones with my skills.

When the department had not expanded too much, we managed get together often; especially during final examinations when external examiners came for viva examination the whole department would collect at one or another faculty member residence for pot luck. Once the exam results were declared, the successful candidates would invited the department members for celebration. I do not know whether the same tradition is being followed now or not. We were close knit, but as the faculty strength increased, jealousy crept in and favoritism started and rivalries started.

Talking bad of a person behind their back and differently in front of them was also an art that some had mastered. One doctor who had recently been superseded by another was sitting in the coffee room with her mentor, who was consoling her by saying that the other fellow did not deserve the promotion, but had got it due to his connection with higher ups etc. A bit later, the successful candidate walked in, and the senior hugged and congratulated him and immediately and started singing his praises, saying "oh I am so happy that you have been successfully selected, -- was getting to big for her boots and deserved a kick on her backside."

It indeed was disgusting to see such double faced people, and somehow, there was no shortage of such people at the institution, and people like me were becoming a minority. A rumor circulated that Dr. Singh was planning to leave for an assignment in Libya; with the pending retirement of Dr. Varma, I was next in seniority, and I suddenly found myself at the centre of attention of such persons, luckily for a short while since Dr. Harivir Singh did not move to Libya. There was a rumor that one faculty member in anesthesiology was having an affair with a surgical colleague, and although people talked so nicely in front of her, they called her dirty names when she was not around.

I too had my fair share of controversies, despite not wanting to be dragged in. Earlier, the post of Associate Professor in our department had fallen vacant, and one of my senior colleagues did not apply for the same as she was not interested in working at the Institute any longer. It was only after assurances from her that I applied. However, on the day of interview, even without applying, she was called from home and offered the job, leaving me with no other option but to go to court. I also represented to the then health minister who was really disgusted with the administration and cancelled the interview. I do not blame my colleague with whom I was always very friendly and still am, and I think it was under pressure from her husband our own head who wanted to rehabilitate her, that this was done.

There was one particular junior faculty member from my department who used to come often to our place. He persuaded my husband to buy a piece of land alongside some land he was buying. While making the payments he was short of money and borrowed 10,000 Rs in cash from my husband, which has not been returned till to date. Not only this, he quietly grabbed our land and started construction on it; luckily we found out in time and had to approach courts for relief.

Chapter 17

PGI was set up with three specific mandates i.e. providing quality care to patients, training and teaching of young postgraduate doctors and performing quality research. Therefore, apart from a very busy routine and emergency clinical work, in this renowned teaching and research place we all had to teach and train junior doctors who had been selected for postgraduation, deliver lectures and present our research work at various fora.

Unfortunately, as the number of faculty grew, so did their personal ambitions, leading to a pool of doctors who only had their own interests in mind, often guided by seniors or those in the administration, possibly with the policy of divide and rule. It was difficult to recognize genuine persons who had no vested interests; true academicians and sincere workers were becoming a rarity. Mediocrity was rapidly becoming the norm; a few persons who were not allowed to continue their residency in Western systems were appointed as faculty and they talked as if they had achieved some sort of greatness by working outside, not realizing that everyone knew what the reality was. There was one surgeon who always came out of the OT saying that this had been the most difficult case he had ever encountered, even if it was a simple one. Another one was very fond of a particular anesthesiologist and made her work overtime by saying that she was the only one who could take care of his complicated risky patients.

But then this was a general attitude in our country where even people like Hargobind Khurana, who got the Nobel Prize, could not get a job in India.

Possibly, we should have also been boot lickers to get ahead at PGI, but this was something that neither my husband nor I could stoop to; we suffered because of this. In 1985, a post of Professor was created in Surgery and despite being a clear choice for the job, my husband was sidetracked and another selected. He represented in court against this, and all hell broke loose for us, and we were harassed at every conceivable opportunity since we had dared to take on the establishment. His own 'close friends' in the department deserted us, planted stories and frivolous complaints against him; people who had been so close to us and visited us often, some even having stayed with us when we were in UK, suddenly became the worst kind of enemies one could not even think of but he stuck to his guns and soldiered on since they really had no substance in them.

In 1988 the post of Professor in Neurosurgical Anesthesiology fell vacant after Professor YS Verma superannuated. At that time, he and I were the two senior persons who had been working in the neurosurgical unit for a long time and it was understood that being the next senior person and with considerable experience in the specialty, I would have a greater claim on the post. In July 1989 interviews were held and again, as per Institute policy of favoritism and pick and choose, a person seven years my junior and who had never worked in Neuroanesthesiology was selected. I was so disgusted that I gave 24 hours' notice of resignation and never set foot at the department again. My well-wishers were after me to go to the court and seek legal advice, and no doubt I would have won the case hands down because there were many glaring discrepancies in the whole process like an incomplete quorum, ineligible expert and unqualified candidate, but disgusted by the whole episode, I decided to quit. My only disappointment was that my head and close family friend had been a party to this selection and he had totally forgotten how much I had supported him during his time of crisis.

Earlier, in 1985, my husband had been offered the post of Professor and Head of Gastroenterology Surgery at Sanjay Gandhi Postgraduate Institute (SGPGI) at Lucknow but since the hospital had not come up then, he had declined the offer. In 1990, he was approached again to take up the position and I was also selected to join as head of Anesthesiology and Intensive Care. Our children were relatively well settled – my elder son, Amit had joined the Civil Services in 1987 and younger son Robin had joined the Armed Forces Medical College at Pune to pursue his dream of becoming a doctor, and so, given the situation at Chandigarh, we decided to make the move.

PART 4

Sanjay Gandhi Postgraduate Institute (SGPGI), Lucknow

CHAPTER 18

Lucknow is the capital city of Uttar Pradesh and its political hub. Its history can be traced back to ancient times, and it was believed that the city was founded by Lord Rama's brother, Laxman on the banks of the river Gomti. It was called Laxmanpura in those times, and even now, there exists a place called Laxman tila, under which the ancient city is believed to be buried. In 1528, Babur captured it, and later, Akbar made it a part of the Awadh province of his kingdom, and later, under Asafuddaula, it became the capital. The city is famous for its culture and 'tehzeeb', monuments, Mughal architecture and educational institutions. King George's Medical College started here in 1911 as the 4th medical college in India, and there are many other famous institutes here, such as the Birla Institute of Paleobotany, Central Drug Research Institute, etc.

Sanjay Gandhi Postgraduate Institute (SGPGI), Lucknow was the most modern and truly tertiary health care institute in India at that time. The foundation stone of SGPGI was laid in 1980 by then then President of India, Shri N. Sanjeeva Reddy with the mandate to establish a world class center of excellence for medical care, education and research of the highest order and to provide teaching and training opportunities to medical and paramedical workers in super specialties as well as a base for basic and applied medicine with aid and transfer of technology from Japanese International Cooperation Agency (JICA). It was one of the most prestigious projects of the country - I always called it a western hospital on Indian soil. It was extremely well equipped;

anything and everything about which I had only read in books till then was available here.

The Institute was spread over a 550 acre area, situated on the outskirts of Lucknow, about 15 kilometres away from the city centre, Hazrat Ganj. As compared to PGI Chandigarh, this was started as a post-doctoral training institute, i.e. further teaching after obtaining MD or MS in a subject. In the first phase, 5 super specialities were started, with a provision of starting 19 more in the second phase.

The department of Anesthesiology was the largest and catered to all the super specialties of neuro-, cardiac, gastro-, nephro- and endocrinology. An intensive care unit of 56 beds had also been planned under the department of which 30 beds had already been commissioned for general, neuro- and cardiac surgeries.

On reaching SGPGI, for the first two days we stayed at the beautiful guesthouse of the Institute till the trucks with our luggage and furniture arrived. We were allotted a bungalow on campus that was fully furnished and had wall to wall carpeting. It seems that the place had been prepared for the Japanese representatives but they preferred to stay in a smaller compact flat which was easier for them to manage. Since it was very hot at Lucknow, we requested the Institute to get those carpets and furnishing removed since our own furniture and large number of household goods had arrived. There were not many people around, but the place and its people were quite friendly and we began to enjoy our stay. In fact there were many senior and junior faculty members who also had come from Chandigarh and thus it was easy to get adjusted.

My first shock was that there was no job for me due to an administrative fault (inefficiency); someone had complained that there were three experts for the interview for the post of anesthesiology in which I had appeared for instead of two, and I was informed that I would not be able to join my post right away, since there was some administrative mix up and the appointment was under active reconsideration of the authorities on the basis of this complaint; the presence of an extra expert was alleged to have vitiated the interview. Later the whole selections for the department of anesthesiology were cancelled and I had to wait for a fresh selection. I found it rather difficult to accept that if three experts instead of two found the candidates suitable for the posts, the selection ought to have been considered more fair and should have been accepted instead of being scrapped. But those are the ways of administration! The only silver lining over the dark clouds was that this waiting period gave me an opportunity to catch up with my desk work and during this time that I was able to write and publish a book on various difficult anesthetic problems namely "Concepts and Management in Anesthesiology".

Anyway, to cut the story short, after a long wait, I joined the department as Professor and Head and a second shock awaited me on joining. I discovered that the 'so-called' Department of Anesthesiology and Critical Care was indeed critically short of almost everything. There was hardly any office space for the head of the department as well as faculty, no seminar room, no teaching aids, no office staff and only a few OT technicians. All the superspecialty surgical cases were being operated upon in a makeshift day care unit, and the so called critical care was being provided in four unprotected, unsterile rooms attached to these operating rooms. Although the Institute had plans for an office block of our department on a grand scale, the priority was low and the building was not ready. Some construction work had started but to my surprise a large portion of it was already taken over by another department.

My faculty members and I had no place where we could do our own work. There was only one small office room, one computer and its operator and a lower division clerk (LDC), both of whom were rejected by all other departments and dumped here. The meagre departmental staff whiled away their time in idle gossip, but over time, it was a matter of great satisfaction to me that somehow I was able to convince and make them both work sincerely. In times to come, we developed an amicable working relationship and two years later, when the LDC was transferred, he was very reluctant to leave the department. The computer operator stayed with the department till his retirement and I understand that he was later re-employed. Our peon was Mr. Brij Lal who was not well educated, and it was a project explaining daily work to him! A few days later, Mr. Ram Prasad was allotted to the department as another peon, but unfortunately, due to some animosity, some miscreants beheaded him one day when he was going back from work. He had a young wife and children, and to help her, we all contributed money and also requested the administration to employ her in place of Ram Prasad, which they ultimately did.

I had to make umpteen visits between my cubby hole and the Director's office and write multiple requests for a few rooms for the department, and eventually a few rooms in E block on the ground floor were allotted to the department. I would like to thank Prof. KN Agrawal, the then Director of SGPGI for the same. We were also given some office furniture which had been already bought by the Institute but had been kept under lock and key. With persistent and sustained efforts, I was able to get additional office man power, Mr. MK Verma as my PA and Mr. Arvind Shrivastava as steno, both of whom proved to be assets to the department.

The main OTs and twelve bed each, General ICU and Cardiac ICU were started in 1993, providing excellent care to patients. The nurses were all trained by our faculty and were not allowed to be transferred to other assignments in the hospital. Monthly and yearly statistics of OT and ICUs were regularly maintained and displayed on the notice board. The number of OT technicians was only 9 when I joined the department, but by 1997 the number had risen to more than 35.

My third and greatest shock was when I came to know that the specialty of Anesthesiology and Critical Care with plans of a 56 bed ICU had been started as a non-teaching, service department. I could not understand the logic of the planners, and realized that my specialty would not progress if the members were not in touch with the latest developments and recent advances in the specialty. Anesthesiology was introduced in 1847, and since then, teaching and research had been going on, with the resultant many surgical feats that could not have been achieved without advances in Anesthesiology, but here, at SGPGI even when the 21st century was approaching, the department was nonacademic and was to provide service only! This was the greatest shock to me, and I was determined to make my department a teaching one, and also one of the best in the country.

Hence, my first priority was to make the department a teaching one. There were more than 10 faculty members with a teaching designation, but they had nothing to teach. Due to some strange reason or perhaps deliberately, appointments of the faculty members had been made at the junior most level of Assistant Professors and lecturers. Before I had joined, the senior most faculty member in my department was an Assistant Professor who had had no say in any administrative matter and was made to sign on dotted lines, but I must admit that he had been able to provide excellent clinical services to various departments.

CHAPTER 19

Given the situation of being a non-academic department, I started daily academic sessions. I still remember the first academic session held after my joining, where I made one of the senior residents, Dr. Monica talk on a topic of importance. There was no seminar room available to us and the class was held in a small room in the day care unit where we did not even have enough chairs to accommodate all of us. During the discussions, I had commented on a very important aspect of one of the drugs but Dr. Mukesh, a faculty member, was not convinced by what I had said. Straight after class, he went to the library to check my statement which turned out to be absolutely correct; from that day onwards he has always held me in high esteem. This was the start of a regular teaching program in the department which initially some faculty were reluctant to attend as they had been enjoying a leisurely life with no teaching sessions and starting OT at their own will, but everyone soon got used to these academic sessions and OTs starting on dot of nine.

Although teaching sessions became regular, the department still remained a non-teaching one, and it was becoming increasingly difficult to retain senior residents because they had no chance of taking up any teaching assignments later since they could not get certificate of working in a teaching department which, as per Medical Council of India rules, was absolutely essential for a job in a medical college or institute; I mooted the idea of post-doctoral certificate courses (PDCC) in cardiac and neuro-anesthesiology. After many discussions with the then

Director, obstacles, struggles and harassment my proposal was discussed threadbare in many committees, sub committees, the Academic board, Governing body and Institute body and finally we were allowed to start the certificate courses. This was the first time in India when such structured specialized course in Anesthesiology had been started anywhere in the country. The first batch cleared the examination in 1994 and it was a proud moment for me when the candidates were immediately accepted as faculty at AIIMS, New Delhi and one of them later went on to head cardiac anesthesiology there.

SGPGI administration had also planned for an intensive care unit of 56 beds which at that time was the largest in the country. In the first phase of the institute five tertiary care super specialties namely cardiac, gastro, urology, neuro and endocrinology had been started and each was to have its own intensive care facility under the care of anaesthesiologist. When I took over, I was surprised to see that four separate rooms were being used for seriously ill patients as a makeshift arrangement for intensive care in the day care unit of SGPGI and doctors and nurses were having a trying time looking after the patients in four different rooms and there was no provision for the attendants to even sit somewhere. Through my sustained efforts and with chief engineer Mr. Abidi's help that I was able to convince the administration to get our block constructed quickly and we then shifted the ICU and OTs to the main block in 1993. Twelve ICU beds were made available for each super specialty and all of them were fully equipped, the patients were looked after the specialty anaesthesiologist. All kinds of gadgets were made available for managing and monitoring patients, and most patients who had undergone major surgeries were put on assisted ventilation at least for twenty four hours and were given pain relief infusion pumps which delivered measured amounts of pain relieving drugs constantly. We were the first to start doing percutaneous tracheostomy.

In addition, just outside the intensive care unit, in a large room, arrangements were also made with facilities for the patient's attendants to rest. Entry to the ICU was restricted, and only one visitor was allowed for few minutes, that too fully gowned and masked. At the entry to ICU ultra violet lights were installed to avoid infection.

All faculty members were encouraged to attend National and International conferences; I still remember that Dr. AK Baronia was the first person who attended a conference in Bangalore in 1992 after making slides and rehearsing them with me. Drs. AK Baronia, Mukesh Tripathy and Atul Gaur presented papers at the International conference at Glasgow in 1993, and by 1998, all faculty members had attended various conferences. For the International Conference at Glasgow, SGPGI administration was not willing to provide financial support to four members from the same department, so in order to let them go, I withdrew my own name; this created a lasting bond with my faculty that has endured even till today. Unfortunately, SGPGI did not provide financial support for residents to attend conferences at that time, and I had to raise a separate departmental fund for this purpose and ensured that senior residents would attend, at least, the national conferences. During my tenure I was able to send all faculty members to attend international conferences.

We also organized a number of CMEs and workshops. Initially, this too was a project as none of the faculty members till then had any experience of organizing a conference or had delivered any lecture. In fact one of them on the day of first CME in 1992 feigned illness just before his lecture was due and had to be forced to participate! A few years later, I was pleasantly surprised to listen to him deliver an excellent talk at one of the conferences and then I knew that my aggression at that time had paid off well. The department organized an Indo-US workshop in 1995 that was attended by teachers from USA, UK, and Japan and senior teachers from all over India. I think that it was the first time in our country that live demonstration of various techniques was shown to the participants through video conferencing, and later this became a norm at many workshops and conferences.

By 1995, the department became known well nationally and internationally. World Anesthesiology News also published an article about the department in 1995, and slowly, we started receiving enquiries from Middle Eastern countries regarding Anaesthesiology training at SGPGI. I also realized that for the department to flourish further, my younger faculty colleagues needed to undergo training and establish themselves professionally. It gives me a great pleasure to mention here that due to my personal contacts I was also able to arrange for a one year training in Anesthesiology, Intensive care and Cardiac Anesthesiology each for Drs. AK Baronia, Mukesh Tripathy, Susheel Ambesh and Prabhat Tiwari at Royal Victoria Hospital, Belfast. For this, I would like to thank Prof. RSJ Clark, Prof. RK Mirakhur, Prof. Morale Lyons and Prof. IM Bali for accepting them and training them at Belfast. Dr. PK Singh and Dr. KC Pant went to Japan for training, and Dr. Atul Gaur was awarded the Commonwealth Scholarship for training in UK. Dr Gaur would have been an asset for the department, but unfortunately, as is wife (a radiologist) could not get a job at SGPGI and they both shifted to UK; they both have done extremely well and Atul is now a renowned author, especially on pain management, and is a sought after faculty all over the world.

All members were encouraged to attend conferences and CMEs at various places and slowly, we became well known in our circles. I too, was invited at various places and received orations and recognition for my work – I was awarded the prestigious Venata Rao Oration and gold medal, the Pandey oration, and invited to various places in India and abroad. In the bicentenary celebrations of RVH, I delivered a talk; in Japan, I met Prof. Starzl, the famous liver transplant surgeon.

There were no scientific publications from the department before my joining, and by the time I left, in 1998, we had 59 original and 7 review articles that had been published in National and International journals of repute such as BJA, Anaesthesiology, Anesthesiology, American Journal of Anesthesiology, Journal of Cardiac Anesthesiology, etc.

It is also a matter of great pride and satisfaction to me, that by the time I left SGPGI in 1998, the department was accorded approval for starting MD course in Anesthesiology by the Medical Council of India. It is a matter of great pride that 3 of the departmental faculty members, namely Dr. PK Singh, Dr. Mukesh Tripathy and Dr. AK Baronia who were initially a non-teaching faculty in a service department are now the directors of newly opened AIIMS at various places.

On the social front too, SGPGI was a friendly place, and I was an active participant in various activities of the SGPGI club of which I was elected President along with Dr. Hukku as secretary. We organized many melas, ladies and children's programs and other such activities at the SPGPGI club – I even wrote a play that was enacted by the children. Professor Das had taken a video of that play, and I hope he still has it! All festivals were celebrated with great pomp and show, and since the then Director of the Institute did not accede to our request for funding, we all chipped in and burnt effigies of Ravana, his brother and son on Dussehra.

CHAPTER 20

As Anesthesiologists, we have access to a large number of drugs that can be dangerous to life, some can paralyze and some can even cause instantaneous death. Given the stresses of our work as well as easy access, addiction to such drugs can become a real problem; I have seen two of the doctors who became addicts and one who committed suicide because of this habit.

At SGPGI, there was a very intelligent faculty member in our department, who, unfortunately, was addicted to marijuana. Although I tried to communicate the same to his wife, she was unwilling to accept the truth; if she had helped, the man would have beaten the habit and been an asset for the department. Unfortunately this was not to be,

There had been a similar instance at PGI Chandigarh where one of our senior residents had a similar problem and it was one of the bright nurses in the recovery room who brought this to my notice. She had observed that this man was repeated asking for morphine ampoules for his patients and often looked dopey; she also knew that morphine was generally not used for neurosurgical patients. After it was brought to my attention, I started observing his behavior closely and noticed that he often had dressings applied to his elbow and left hand, and when asked about them, he would be evasive and tell a different story every day, a needle pick while sewing, scratches from his young baby, pet dog and so on. When I could wait no longer, I confronted him in my office and after much coughing he admitted that he had become a morphine addict. He was taking the drug three times normal and could not manage without it and his wife was not aware of this. Finally, he admitted under Psychiatry for deaddiction, and later, was advised to leave the specialty and work in a branch where there would be no access to such drugs.

As a departmental head one also becomes privy to non-professional, personal and sensitive problems of members. At SGPGI, there was a fair share of such problems, from depression to dowry related issues and even sexual harassment complaints, and I always tried to do my best to sort them out.

No doubt, while at SGPGI I had my share of stresses and frustrations but I am happy to see that my perseverance paid off well. I spent the best and most fruitful years of my life at the Institute, doing work that I now realise I would have been unable to do if I had stayed on at PGI. My husband too, did tremendously well in his professional career, starting MCh in Gastrointestinal Surgery and building a world renowned department at SGPGI. When we superannuated in 1998, there were very few departments in the country that could compare to ours, and we were considered amongst the best in the world. In 1994 we started structured certificate courses in Cardiac and Neuro-anesthesiology. The syllabi for the same were carefully worked out by the department and later on approved by the Governing body of the Institute. Candidates for these courses were selected after a thorough written and oral examination and had to go through a rigorous schedule. They were awarded a certificate after assessment by external examiners in theory as well as in practical; these later became DM Course in Neuroanesthesiology (in 1996) and Cardiac Anesthesiology (around 2002), much before PGI.

The success of any training program can be assessed by the benefits of the trainees. Although, initially, I had to face tremendous difficulties and opposition in starting these courses, the results have borne fruit, and I am really happy to say that almost all of the trainees from SGPGI have been able to secure faculty positions/consultancy at prestigious Institutes and Colleges of the Country such as AIIMS, SGPGIMS, Sri Chitra, KGMC, Apollo Hospital, etc. and even abroad.

When we superannuated in 1998, we were given many farewell dinners and parties by our colleagues and residents, and I must say that I have spent the best years of my life at SGPGI. I am still in touch with most of my faculty, nurses and office staff.

It is a matter of pride for me that the department of Anesthesiology at SGPGI started an oration in my name – I was invited to deliver the inaugural oration, but due to the Covid pandemic and subsequent lockdown, it had to be postponed.

The department is now reaping the benefits of my toil and I am sure wish that the present head of the department will take it to even greater heights, and I wish him and all faculty, staff, and students the very best of luck in all walks of life.

After a brief stint in the private sector, we settled down in Panchkula where we had constructed a house in 1983. My husband, at the request of Dr. Kak, our old family friend, joined a new and upcoming medical college in Chandigarh where Dr. Kak was the Director-Principal, to streamline the department of Surgery. I decided not to join Private Practice in Anesthesiology, and stayed home with family and grandchildren, working during the mornings doing charitable clinics (providing health care to the needy poor), writing a health column for one of the vernacular magazines for over ten years, and published children's story books which have been now been translated into English,

Punjabi, Tamil and other regional languages by National Book Trust of India.

This is the story of my life.

PART 5

A brief history of Anesthesiology, especially in India

Chapter 21

Although the credit of introducing anesthesiology to modern medical practice goes to WTG Morton, it was Gardner Quincy Colton from US of America who initially thought of pain relief during surgery and was the first person to have demonstrated the hypnotic effects of nitrous oxide (laughing gas), in 1844 at Connecticut. A local dentist Horace Wells was also present during this demonstration and observed that a shop assistant hurt his leg under the influence of the gas but did not feel any pain. It is believed that Wells persuaded Colton to try the gas for dental extractions and offered himself as a patient. Wells was so impressed by the effects of the gas that he started using it for his patients regularly. Unfortunately when he tried to convince and demonstrate these effects to a large gathering of students of Harvard medical school he failed miserably and was booed out. This left such a serious effect on him that he became mentally unbalanced and an addict and later committed suicide by cutting his own femoral artery.

The first successful demonstration of anesthesia using ether was held at Massachusetts General Hospital (USA) on 16th October 1846 by WTG Morton for removal of a jaw tumor. Morton himself was a dentist, and partner of Horace Wells, and had been present at the time of demonstration of nitrous oxide when Wells had failed. He later separated from Wells and started experimenting with ether which he had named as Litheon to keep the identity of its chemical nature a secret. Following the successful demonstration of ether anesthesia by Morton, the news travelled far and wide and the drug became popular instantaneously in UK, continental Europe and Australia and even in India. It is unfortunate that Morton did not get any recognition for his discovery during his life time, but now, he known as the father of present day anesthesiology.

In 1847 Dr. JY Simpson an Edinburgh obstetrician, introduced Chloroform in clinical practice, and this agent became very popular because of its property of inducing anesthesia smoothly and rapidly. Though anesthesia with ether was far safer than chloroform, somehow general public was more aware about chloroform, probably because it had been used on Queen Victoria in 1853 during childbirth of her eighth child Prince Leopold. The drug became so popular that Anesthesiologists became known as chloroformists and even today, after more than 170 years, the name of drug is known even though the drug is no more in use.

This was followed by rapid advances in local, spinal and general anesthesia, and soon, many new and safe local anesthetics were available. It has only been the advances in anesthesiology that have led to advances in surgery, and anesthesiology is a well-established specialty in itself today – a good surgeon always knows the value of a good anesthesiologist!

In UK, before the discovery of anesthesiology, all large hospitals had only one operating session per week and the maximum number of operations was performed at Glasgow. This number started to rise once anesthesiology started gaining popularity, and by 1862, the number of sessions at rose to 7 per week. By the year end, St. Bartholomew's Hospital had performed 327 operations, Guy's 541, and Leeds, 211 operations; the number kept rising as the popularity of anesthesiology grew.

India, one of the well-established colonies of the British Empire, was quick to receive information of both - the introduction of anesthesiology, as well as of training and teaching. India can boast of a significant contribution towards the development of anesthesiology - while there are reports from pre-ether era describing conduct of surgery using opium, wine, Indian hemp, etc., Indians were quick to adopt newer anesthetic agents. The first administration of either anesthesia in India was on 22nd of March, 1847, in Medical College Hospitals, Calcutta, under the supervision of Dr. O'Shaughnessy, the surgeon, within just five months of administration of first ether anesthesia in the world (on October 16th 1846). Similarly, the first chloroform anesthesia in India was administered on January 12th 1884

Chloroform anesthesia was mired in controversies because of complications. Edwards Lawrie in 1888 in Hyderabad formed the "First Hyderabad Chloroform Commission" and reported its safety. A "Second Hyderabad Chloroform Commission" was formed with a representative from Lancet and it concluded that chloroform was not directly injurious to the heart and killed only by its effect on respiration. t is during the working of the second commission, that Dr. Roop Bai Furdoonji, perhaps the first Indian anesthesiologist came under spotlight. She worked with Edward Lawrie and Thomas Brunton and assisted the commission's work which consisted of administration of chloroform to human beings and animal experiments. She later received part of her training in Edinburgh and worked as a full time anesthesiologist at the British Residency Hospital in Hyderabad,

The Hyderabad Medical School was the first to start training in Anesthesiology in 1890. The earliest document regarding instructions in anesthesiology is reported from Calcutta in 1906. The first chair of anesthesiology was created at Oxford in 1937, occupied by Sir Robert McIntosh and the first examination of Diploma in UK was also held in 1937; Diploma in Anesthesiology in India was started in 1946. In the initial stages, one year training leading to diploma was thought to be sufficient, but as time progressed, it was realized that the anesthesiologists required sound knowledge of Physiology, Pharmacology and Physics in relation to the day to day management of patients, as well as the use of anesthesiology equipment. Therefore, limited one year training was thought to be inadequate. The first fellowship examination in Anesthesiology of the Royal College, UK was held in 1953, and India started its MD/MS program soon after, in 1955; the first PhD in anesthesiology, if I recall correctly, was from Bombay. Dr. D Sharma was the first veterinary anesthesiologist who did his PhD from PGI Chandigarh in the mid 70's.

It was in 1944 that anesthesiologists attending a surgical conference at Mumbai (Bombay) thought of forming a common platform for exchange of scientific views, which was consolidated following "Ether Day" celebrations in October of 1946. With continued efforts of leading anesthesiologists of India, the Indian Society Anesthesiologists was born on 30th December 1947 as a joint organization with the Surgical-Obstetric Society of India. The founder of members of the society were Dr. GS Ambardekar, Dr. VB Bhargava, Dr. JG Mehta and Dr. Talwalkar G.S. (all from Bombay), Dr. HG Barat, Dr. SK Chatterjee and Dr. PB Sur (from Calcutta), Dr. SK Bakshi, Dr. PD Dhameja and Dr. Satyaendra Singh (from Delhi), Dr. Chandrasekhar (Madras), Dr. N Prasad (Patna) and Dr. MN Desai (who was the founder President). The first conference was held on 23rd to 24th of December, 1949 at Seth GS Medical College, Bombay.

In 1953 the society started publishing its official journal "Indian Journal of Anesthesia": with Dr. MC Gangule as the first editor of the journal; since 1959, it is published quarterly.

In 1956, the Indian Society of Anesthesiologists (ISA) joined the World Federation of Societies of Anesthesiologists (WFSA) as a founder member. In 1958, at the 10th Annual Conference at Visakhapatnam, the governing council passed a resolution authorizing different states to form state branches; the first state branch was formed in West Bengal in 1958 and subsequently other states followed.

The emblem of the society was designed by Dr. Badola from Lucknow, and the design was accepted in 1964 and has been used as the logo since. The emblem signifies "the patient's safety through unconsciousness" steered by mythical mermaids (representing anesthesiologists) who have human intelligence as well as the skill of a dolphin in swimming waves that represent unexpected emergences that arise in anesthesiology practice. The dark and light shades represent the sleep and awake states. The motto is 'Eternal Vigilance' whether day or night, further symbolized by the alternate shades; the serpents and rod represent the medical profession.

ISA hosted its first independent Annual National Conference at Hyderabad in 1965 where Prof. Dr. TC Grey and Prof. Dr. R. Macintosh from UK were special invitees.

In September 1978, the 5th Asian-Australian Regional conference was held at New Delhi and the conference was inaugurated by the then President of India. Continuing Medical Education (CME) Programs were started along with the Annual Conference in 1981 at Chandigarh under WFSA initiatives (Dr. TCK Brown).

The South Asian Confederations of Anesthesiologists (SACA) was formed in November 1991 and Dr. (Mrs.). VM Divekar was selected as the first SACA

President. SACA meets once in two years in one of the member countries at Bangladesh/Sri Lanka /India /Nepal/ Maldives. In 1999 Chennai (Madras) India, hosted the SACA meet.

1972 and 1997 were the Silver Jubilee and Golden Jubilee years of the formation of the formation of ISA respectively which were celebrated at Trivandrum (1972) and Delhi (1997). The Silver Jubilee and Golden Jubilee Conferences were held in 1975 and 2002 at Madras and Coimbatore respectively.

It is now standard in our country to have a three year MD program with examination as the basic qualification in Anesthesiology. This is followed further by supervised training as a senior resident in a teaching hospital, especially if one wishes to take up an academic profession. In most of the countries of the world a similar program of three to four year exists, and in some countries the final year is reserved for training in super specialties.

Anesthesiology, once a technical procedure carried out by a person with no knowledge of human body and its requirements has now progressed and THE ART OF ANESTHESIA HAS NOW BEEN REPLACED BY SCIENCE OF ANESTHESIOLOGY. The sphere of activities is no longer confined to the four walls of operation theatres, and the present day anesthesiologist is involved in pain management, CPR, critical care, cardiac cath labs, MRI, ultrasound guided nerve blocks, and other such specialized techniques. He/She has to be a pulmonary physician as well.

We are now living in the era of renal, hepatic, cardiac, lung transplantation and perhaps would soon require learning anesthesiology for outer space as well. In the last two decades the importance of super specialization in surgery has been realized and large number of super specialty hospitals have also come up in the government and the private sector, bringing me to the million dollar question- should we have post-doctoral courses in the super specialties of anesthesiology? It is essential to consider whether the objective of training in anesthesiology should remain the same under all circumstances or should they change? The "jack of all trades" approach of the yesteryear is not possible today in the same way as a general surgeon cannot be asked to perform cardiac, neuro, pediatrics, urological or complex gastrointestinal surgical procedures. There is no doubt in my mind that if all the anesthesiologists could work in all super specialties there could be a distinct advantage of all call schedules, convenience, work sharing and sense equality, and above all, better patient care. But at the same time, it is essential that the anesthesiologist who is working in Cardiac, Neuro or Pediatric specialties is well versed in problems of these specialties where the intricacies of drug therapy and interactions, disease process and specific events need coordination and facilitation amongst the team. If the anesthesiologist's only activity is to carry out the directives of the surgeons then super specialty training may not be necessary, but if she/he is a real member of the team providing specialized care, participating in thinking, decision making and carrying them out super specialization become essential

Dr. P Mazumder took the lead in starting a combined one year training program in Neuro- and Cardiac anesthesiology at Sri Chitra Tirunal Institute, Thiruvananthapuram where candidates spent six months in each specialty. Nizam's Institute at Hyderabad soon followed suit, but advances in super specialties necessitated an increased training in the respective specialties, and only six month training did not seem adequate. As I mentioned before, we were the first in the country to start structured courses separately in Cardiac and Neuro anesthesiology (in 1994) that later became full-fledged DM courses.

In more than almost hundred and seventy-five years after the magnificent discovery of anesthesiology we have now moved from a brief, one day training to comprehensive teaching in super specialties. It must be realized that we are not training our young anesthesiologists for today or tomorrow but in the space age of 21st century to be able to handle any clinical situation 20 to 30 years later. The future of the specialty depends not on more gadgets, monitors, or drugs, but on dedicated clinical anesthesiologists who have a sound knowledge of the specialty and can handle situations with rational judgement.

You may be surprised to note that an institution like PGI Chandigarh did not have chair in specialty till as late as 1977 and the department was headed by a pediatric surgeon for many years. Dr. Harivir Singh was the first chair at PGI, and over time, the specialty of anesthesiology has grown tremendously in India and has now achieved an independent status in all medical colleges and hospitals. The National Academy of Medical Sciences, New Delhi is also imparting DNB degree after examination.

Printed by Libri Plureos GmbH in Hamburg, Germany